Expert Success

My Proven 3-Step Formula To Becoming An Overnight Authority In Any Industry

Daniel Wagner

British Library Cataloguing in Publication Data.

A catalogue record for this book is available from the British Library.

Paperback Edition ISBN 978-0-9576557-0-6

Hardcover Edition ISBN 978-0-9576557-1-3

Digital Edition ISBN 978-0-9576557-2-0

Expert Success At a Glance

Introduction to Expert Success

A Different World...

It's not just a different world, it's a totally different economy to the one we grew up in - and if we don't pay attention to the fast changing world around it, we'll be left behind. But I don't want to start this book by getting you worried or concerned, because this new economy holds a tremendous opportunity for anyone who cares to pay attention and take action.

I want to start with a bold claim: 'This book can make you wealthy, give you more time, more freedom and create more meaning in your life...'

I guess I've got your attention. A book that can make you wealthy, happy and free? Give me a break! Yet this is exactly what happened to me when I applied the knowledge shared in this book to my own life.

It took me from being broke and in a job I hated to making hundreds of thousands of pounds, going on holiday many times a year and most importantly lead me to a life I love waking up to every day! I have found purpose! Admittedly - finding it was accidental, but crafting it and teaching it has been nothing short of amazing!

I have taught many 'ideas' and 'strategies' over the years, but never have found one that not only resonated with so many people, it is also a business model that almost anyone can copy and get great results - fast.   And for the last 18 months I started teaching this formula to my students in the Expert Success Academy and shared it with other business owners with mind boggling results!

I have published the first version of this book - the 'Expert Success Formula' back in March 2012 and have since revised it 5 times! To be sure, I tested the simple 3-step formula for a few months. I added more tips and shortcuts to the process and every few months I collected more success stories!

So much so that we have published a book called 'Expert Success Stories' this year just to be able to share the amazing stories of everyday people who decided to change their lives and have more money, more time and more purpose!

But let me introduce myself. My name is Daniel Wagner, I am from Austria and I came to the UK in 1995. Not long ago I lived in Slough working part time for Domino's delivering pizzas, now I have multiple businesses and I am a highly paid expert flying round the world delivering my knowledge on authentic personal branding and expert positioning.

What happened in between those two extremes is another book (If you want to read the whole painful story, you can get my first book 'My Journey and the Machine'), but to sum it up I went through many mind numbing and unrewarding 'jobs' and enterprises to get to where I am today.

I am not a billionaire, but I have a few properties, I own stakes in a few profitable businesses (mostly students of mine I helped), I absolutely love what I do, I look after my health and family and I have a few good friends and a wonderful partner. Life is good!

But best of all, I've been able to help hundreds of people take charge of their own lives by starting their own business or making more money and give them new inspiration and meaning. 'Expert Success' is how I did it. I passionately believe that Expert Success and the knowledge shared is a toolset that creates a better world - one Expert at a time.

I believe that the world needs Experts, it needs Leadership, it needs people like you and me to step up to the plate, telling their story, sharing their message and creating micro businesses to save the economy. We can't rely on governments or companies to look after us and our families. We have to do it ourselves. So it's time to stand up and take your life in your own hands!

I can't promise you that'll be easy. But I can promise you it'll be rewarding! Independence, freedom, purpose. These are the ingredients of an empowered life. And if you apply just some of the ideas from this book then you'll have more money and more time available to spend on the things you love! Can you imagine making twice or three times the money working less and doing what you love? That is what Expert Success is about!

In the last 12 months I lost both my parents and I just wish they had seen Expert Success grow to be a global influence and movement. It's too late for them but it's not too late for you. Life's short.

Daniel Wagner

Daniel Wagner

London, June 2013

PS: In the first chapter I'll quickly explain some of the fundamentals you absolutely must know about.

Understanding the 'Expert Industry'

How to Become Part of this Multi-Billion Dollar Industry

I need to quickly explain a few terms to illustrate some of the phenomenons I observed that will allow you to dramatically increase your paycheck and live a life you love. The first one is the 'Expert Industry'.

There is a growing market and opportunity (I'll explain some of the reasons behind this over the next few pages) for people to become the 'go-to person'. Everywhere you go so-called 'experts' are called to the rescue. They are authorities in their respective fields, they are the published faces of whole industries and they are well paid with money and attention.

What most don't know though that there is no club to join, there is no certification to pass and there is no degree to be had. It is a weird and seemingly random collection of attributes that is needed to make our society believe and have society bestow upon a mere mortal to be an 'Expert'. Once you know what these things are, you can adorn yourself with the attributes and bingo - you de facto have become an 'Expert'.

This might baffle you - you might even think that it is not right or unfair to just take advantage of this 'imperfect' market. I think it's wonderful! Haven't you always wondered how some people out there ended up being 'gurus' and highly-paid 'experts', when in fact you know as much (or more!) and could do the same job (or better!).

What has driven the massive growth of this 'Expert Industry' is the internet and technological revolution that has allowed literally anyone to appear to be an expert. Now - just to be clear - I do not advocate 'pretending' to know your stuff, but I am advocating to do whatever you can to be perceived as an expert and to get noticed! In the past (only a decade or so ago) this game was reserved to a lucky few - connected by school ties or elite country clubs - now the doors are wide open! The playing fields have been leveled! Your chance to join the game!

I believe we're looking at a unique time in the history of mankind. Technology and the internet have connected the world for the first time. Production and distribution are no longer the driving forces of the economy. We have moved from a production to a knowledge based economy, and you only have to look at the FTSE100 or NASDAQ to see who's quoted today compared to 50 years ago! It's about services and information!

Look at the latest bunch of millionaires and billionaires. They are not steel tycoons! They all operate in software or service-based industries. That opens incredible opportunities for all of us who are willing to move with the times.

Joining the expert industry is especially easy and lucrative and fast in any area where you can sell information or information products or any area that includes teaching, coaching or any other form of knowledge transfer from events to online membership sites.

I do think though that there is only a short window of opportunity and you'll have to move fast! I mentioned earlier that 'expert status' is not awarded. It is indeed 'claimed' - which means it's down to you and you alone to go out there, put your stake in the ground and to claim what is rightfully yours. So if you have knowledge and skills to solve problems for people, then you can claim your space in this expert industry and become the leader of a micro-tribe and micro-economy will be born. Join the industry and claim your space before it's too late!

How to exploit the 'Expert Success Matrix'

In every field of knowledge or in any industry there seems to always be a handful of people who make the bulk of the money. Have you noticed? From Hollywood actors to chefs, from pop music to football, there are only a few who know how to make the big money, while the rest are just getting by.

I've called this phenomenon of universal market dynamics the 'Expert Success Matrix'. The matrix though doesn't just explain the disproportionate distribution of wealth, it also highlights some other key distinction you can benefit from.

I'll build the matrix for you step-by-step, just like I do it when I present this concept to an audience.

First of all, in any field, market or industry there's a distribution of people where most are perceived to know very little about a topic, and a small number of people are perceived to know a lot. (Figure 1)

Please notice that I have used the phrase 'perceived to know' not 'know'. The reason is that the way we look at the position of a person on the matrix is pretty much exclusively based on his expert status, not his true knowledge or ability to perform a certain task or use his skills.

You might find this shocking or unfair - but if this is a truism across the world, I suggest to use it to your advantage instead of complaining about the status quo. I am all for educating a market, but I am not gonna fight a universally accepted opinion if I can avoid it.

The Expert Success Matrix™

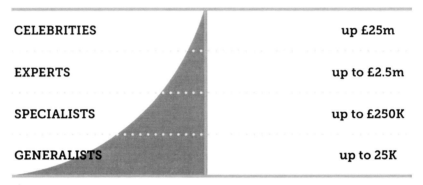

CELEBRITIES	**up £25m**
EXPERTS	**up to £2.5m**
SPECIALISTS	**up to £250K**
GENERALISTS	**up to 25K**

(Figure1) The 'Expert Success Matrix' shows that most people are perceived to know little or nothing about a given subject, being at the bottom of the matrix, while only a small number are perceived to be 'Experts' and 'Celebrities'- positioned at the top of the matrix. On the right hand side you see the yearly earning potentials per segment.

The next part of the matrix shows how the money and attention in any industry is distributed. It is pretty much directly opposite, meaning that a small amount of people get the 'big money', while the majority has to fight for scraps. (see figure 2).

We can therefore deduce that what I call 'Expert Positioning' - the perceived status of a person which is only loosely connected with their true skill or knowledge - is directly link to the amount of money available to an individual. It's important that you understand this is not inked to their true expertise or ability to perform a given task - it's based on their position and the associated perceived expertise/ability (Figure 2).

The Expert Success Matrix™

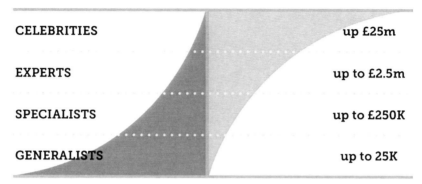

CELEBRITIES	**up £25m**
EXPERTS	**up to £2.5m**
SPECIALISTS	**up to £250K**
GENERALISTS	**up to 25K**

(Figure 2) The money distribution in any market is inverse to the position along the 'Expert Position Axis'. Like it or not, you can observe this to be true in any market or field from science to art to all service professionals.

Now that we have agreed on these two facts being connected - the amount of people and the amount of money, let's look at the effect of this correlation by using a real world example. Let's look at John, a health coach, passionate and knowledgable about nutrition who helps people with their diet.

John loves what he does and he is good at it. He knows his stuff! If you were to put him on the matrix though, he would only find himself at the bottom quarter of the 'Expert Positioning Axis', making him - at least in expert terms - a nobody! Sorry John. (Figure 3)

The Expert Success Matrix™

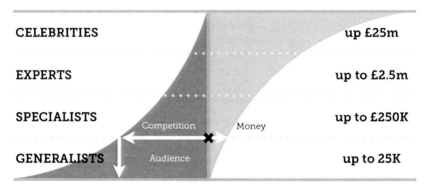

(Figure 3). The 3 problems associated with a low place on the 'Expert Positioning Axis' of the 'Expert Success Matrix'. Big competition, small audience and a struggle to survive.

Now John might not care where we put him along the 'Expert Positioning Axis' in the 'Expert Success Matrix', but there are three problems with John's position.

There are thousands of people positioned where he is, (the competition) making John in expert terms a 'Generalist'.

Because of his position John can't reach many people (his audience) and can therefore only help relatively few people

And the money available in the marketplace for that level of expert position (the non-specialist) - will keep John struggling to survive - which in turn will create resentment and ultimately result in John not enjoying what he does!

The Expert Success Matrix™

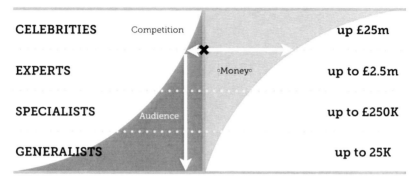

(Figure 4). The higher up on the 'Expert Positioning Axis' of the 'Expert Success Matrix' you are, the better. Just some of the rewards include less or no competition, more and better clients and a lot more money.

Before we discuss what John can do to fix this, let's first establish why it's so much better to be the 'Expert' or 'Celebrity' in your industry.

Let me highlight an incredible side effect of being in the top 10% of the positioning axis. I mentioned little competition, but at this stage of the game you have pretty much NO competition. Because at this level personality and who you are becomes more important than what you can do!

I can illustrate this with an example from celebrity chefs here in the UK. Do you think Heston Blumenthal and Delia Smith are really in competition? Of course not. Their ability to 'make food' is actually not that important. Instead it's about style and personality, values and mission that is now important. This allows them to move into the 'Celebrity' segment of the matrix, where you can form and lead tribes and sell pretty much anything with your name on it.

Now that we've established why you want to be on the top end of the matrix - let's talk about how to get there. What'll surprise you is that it's not difficult to have higher perceived expertise and better positioning if you follow a few simple rules.

The simple 3 Steps to 'Expert Success'

A Formula to More Money, More Time and More Purpose

The subtitle of this book is called 'My Proven 3-Step Formula to Becoming an Overnight Authority in any Industry' and it promises you 'more money, more time and more purpose'. Becoming an 'Expert' is what this book is all about and you have to simply follow the 3 steps to move 'up the matrix' and reap all the benefits associated with your new position.

I teach the same knowledge outlined in this book in all my courses and coaching programs with consistent and tangible results. From our humble 'Expert Success Gold Coaching' all the way to the lofty heights of the 'Expert Success Mastermind' - the principles of our teaching are always the same and are based on the 3 steps outlined on the next couple of pages. All that changes is the amount of access to either myself or our Expert Success Coaches and the intensity of immersion in the subject matter - and of course, your investment!

I have reverse engineered the most impressive success stories into this formula and what you get in this book is the very same knowledge and the very same distinctions that many of my students have paid tens of thousands of pounds for.

The 3 step formula to Expert Success can benefit literally anybody. I have tested it in a variety of markets and industries, with people from all walks of life and the result has always been the same. More money, more time, more purpose!

There are just three factors to position yourself higher up on the 'Expert Success Matrix', and these three main concepts are very easy to grasp - to implement them will take some time and persistence, but the rewards are worth it!

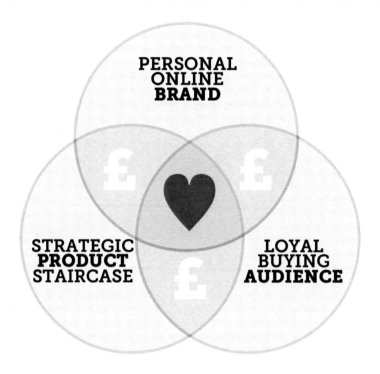

Expert Success is based on 3 overlapping factors. Leave one out, or be out of balance, and you miss the full effect. The heart in the center symbolizes that your work should be driven by passion, and the '£' signs indicate that when these ingredients of the formula are in place, money will follow naturally. The stronger the ingredients, the more money you'll make.

Step 1: an Authentic Personal Brand

How to Position Yourself Online To Be Found

Authentic Personal Branding is about two things. Having an authentic and consistent 'Online Avatar' across different channels and media and 'Being Found'. Today people are googling each others names before even considering doing business with each other and it doesn't take a crystal ball to predict that in the near future you'll be losing out if you don't have a clear online presence. That's why it is so important you decide what you want to be known for, your 'promise' to the market.

The power of branding is not new. It's been documented in many studies and our world is dominated by brands for many reasons. For your 'Expert Success' though I will make a strong and convincing case for a concept I call 'Personal Brand'. It is actually far faster and easier to implement and won't cost you millions of dollars either! Within the 'Personal Brand' concept I want to focus on the 'Online' side of it, where I've found the most immediate results in moving people up the Expert Success Matrix.

Step 2: a Range of Powerful Products

Offer Strategically Sequenced Products and Services

If you want to make money online or offline, you need something to sell (your products or services), but most peoples' concept of making money is firmly rooted around trading their time for money in a job or in their business. The 'Expert Success' model teaches you to create multiple products and/or services from your knowledge or expertise with a focus to have as many of them as possible sold and delivered automatically.

This leverage factor will allow you to break free from the time-for-money restriction of traditional jobs and the old model of the service professional of the last century. The key and goal is to build a strategic sequence of offers that help people and solve their problems.

A handful of strategically sequenced products/services will allow you to multiply your current income manyfold. The near zero cost distribution channels of the internet and technology have made it extremely easy and fast to test, improve and establish high profit information products and services.

Step 3. Cultivate A Buying Audience

How To Build A Loyal Following and Continuously Give Value

This is the part that makes your 'Expert Success' real. This is the 'people' part. It is again down to the internet and the technological advancement that makes it easy and possible to create tribes and communities worldwide at the touch of a button at literally no cost. What's more, you'll only need a handful of loyal followers to make a very decent amount on money!

I'll go through choosing your customer profiles (also referred to as 'customer avatar') and help you find your 'perfect' customer. I've also come to understand a handful of simple strategies of how to cultivate a relationship with your customers that is long lasting and highly profitable.

Most businesses focus too much on expensive lead generation and client acquisition, 'Expert Success' focuses on 'tribe building' - which is the art and science of creating a community that has a strong sense of belonging and protection. We all want to belong, so if you are able to build a group, lead a group and inspire a group you'll cultivate a loyal and dedicated following - and a buying audience.

Why you should become an 'Expert'

I've literally wasted many years of my life, drifting from one unfulfilling job and meaningless work to another, always knowing deep inside that I had something more to give and that I had this great potential. Sadly no one was prepared to pay me for my potential! If you're anything like me, then this will sound familiar. Luckily for me, my life has changed - radically! But I guess you are reading this book because you are looking to fulfill this potential and finally get the reward you want and deserve.

I'm not saying that you can become an Expert overnight, but you'll be amazed that by following the steps in this book that you can quickly and efficiently increase your value in your industry, bringing you more money, more time and more purpose as a direct result of your increased Expert status!

My definition of an Expert includes teaching and leading people. I don't want to think of Experts as scientists or nerds being locked away in some lab. My Experts are people who love people and who go out to spread the word.

I already mentioned this, but you can simply 'claim' your Expert Positioning and don't have to wait for anyone to award you. I have seen this mind shift occur many times and it's an amazing moment for people to recognize they are already Experts, they just have to start letting the world know! I'll talk about the 95:5 formula a bit later, but you'll qualify, I'm sure!

So here are just a few of the juicy benefits of choosing to become an Expert in your industry:

Get paid more

There is literally no glass ceiling of how much you can earn in the Expert industry. I have worked my way from £5/hr (delivering pizzas - clearly not an expert role!) all the way to £3,000 a day (as a marketing consultant). And this is by no means the end!

What's even better is the automated and leveraged income from products and services when you build your business. Let's say you are currently making £20,000 or £30,000 a year, how would you like £200,000 or £300,000 for doing essentially the same thing? I've done it, it's clearly possible!

What about making £500,000 or £1,000,000? I've done it - it's clearly possible!

Do what you love

This one is a stretch for most people. It's hard to believe that you could get paid amazing amounts of money, help people AND do what you love!

You might be shaking your head and think - 'Ok, Dan - I buy the positioning stuff. I also buy the internet magic thing - but LOVING what you do AND make tons of money? You're pushing it.'

I'm just suggesting at this stage that you might have bought into the wrong plan. If you establish your Expert positioning, then life can indeed be a breeze.

For me that was a big one. I really did believe for most of my life that there is what I love doing on one hand and there is work - the stuff that makes me money - on the other hand. Having your cake and eat it - that is just sweet. Expert Success is just that. Sweet! And take it from a guy in his late forties! Life's too short to waste it on something you hate doing!

Attract and get chosen

If you have ever been in a sales role or tried to run your own business, then this is big! I have to just spend a few words to prepare you for the immensity of this concept. The difference between selling and chasing clients compared to clients being attracted to buy from you and being 'chosen' are literally night and day.

The difference in psychology of this is immense. Imagine yourself going from door to door offering your product or service. This is what most people do. Now imagine people coming to you because you are the go-to person in the industry. Which role is more fun and more rewarding?

The begging days are over. Once you're an Expert, people will come and find you. I get invited to speak on Expert Success and Personal Branding all the time! Just a few weeks ago I spoke on stage and was paid a handsome five figure sum loving every moment of it. (that's like 6 months driving round delivering pizzas thank you very much)

Become a Leader in your industry

This is maybe a less obvious benefit and might scare a few folks. I get it. I avoided this one for many years. But it's intrinsically linked with your perception in the market place of being an Expert. We'll talk a lot more about 'vision' and 'mission' later and why that is important, but here is the short summary.

You either lead or you follow. You either play or you watch. And from all the evidence I observed, leaders get paid and get the glory, players have the fun and make the money!

I've done a lot of self development work. Over twenty years of meditation, Tony Robbins, T Harv Eker, Jim Rohn and many more - but running your own business is one of the most intense ways to face yourself and learn about yourself.

It's down to you. It takes a bit of courage to lead and yes - you have responsibility - but I can only tell you from my own experience and the hundreds of people I have helped move into that position that life's far more exciting and fulfilling if you lead!

Can You become a Well Paid 'Expert'?

One of my favourite parts of talking to people or presenting from stage is the topic of 'who can benefit from this Expert Success Formula'? I'm just amazed at how wide-ranging the scope of this formula really is. I know I'm the proverbial 'man with the hammer' - but I truly believe that this knowledge and the concepts of Expert positioning is pretty much universal!

I've seen this knowledge applied to 'new' Experts; literally people who just decided to 'claim' their Expert position on the spot and went on to become well paid and respected authorities in just months!

I've many times seen existing Experts finally get the financial recognition and reward they deserve by assuming their rightful position - not to mention the respect from their families and peers.

This even has created surprising results for employees in the corporate game, employees who have used the three step formula to accelerate their career or leap up the corporate ladder.

You can trawl through a plethora of Expert Success Stories - several of whom we'll refer to in this book. Of course there is now a whole book full of stories called Expert Success Stories!

We have been able to achieve Expert Success for individuals and businesses in many areas, including:

Meditation, Virtual Assistants, Web Design, Renovation, Property Investment, Digital Product Creation, Tennis, Nutrition, Alkaline Diet, Social Media, Public Speaking, Internet Marketing, Business Coaching, Body Transformation, Life Coaching, Pet Grooming, Hair Dressing, Solar Installations, Accountants, Publishers...

… the Expert Success Formula is a flexible and adaptable framework for pretty much anyone.

And if you're already a successful business owner or a budding entrepreneur, I can almost guarantee that you'll explode and fast track your business success… I've seen it happen many times.

So before I get into the more detailed how-to part of this book, let me say a few words of encouragement and gratitude:

I wanted to personally thank you for taking the time to study this material. I know there are many things you could be doing with your time, so I really appreciate it. I'm confident you'll gain some insights. I'm confident you'll have some breakthroughs and 'aha!' moments. And should you choose to apply the learnings, then I am sure you'll see the results very quickly like hundreds before you.

To your own Expert Success, may you have more time and more purpose and make lots of money!

1. Establish a Personal Brand

Establishing a Personal (Online) Brand is one of the cornerstones of lasting Expert Success. It is the first big step to putting your message out there, putting your name out there and showing the world that you 'mean business'. It's as much about leadership as it is about Expert positioning.

Personal Branding is a very different animal to Corporate or Product Branding. Although our job is similar in the sense that every brand tries to establish uniqueness in the market place, our job to be perceived as an Expert or authority is actually a lot easier than, as you already have uniqueness based on you as a person and your history and mix of skills and experience.

'So when will I make all this money you talk about?'

I know that most of you want to get right to the money and product bit, but we just have to get some other bits out of the way. Before we delve into the joys of putting your name and expertise into the stormy waves of the virtual oceans, we got to get some foundational work done.

It'll be fun (kind of) and it'll be over before you know it! And from my experience I can only say that most people who have been through the process found it invaluable or at least useful.

You know by now that Expert Success in the new economy is based on 3 big parts. Every part is furthermore divided into 3 simple chunks.

So big part number one, 'Establish a Personal Online Brand', is divided into three sub sections, 'Clarify Your Vision', 'Create Your Online Avatar' and 'Claim Your Expert Status'.

Some of the questions and chapters speak of starting a business, but I want to encourage and urge existing business owners and established businesses to absorb the concepts and look at this as an opportunity to do some 'day zero thinking'.

1.1 Clarify Your Vision

In this part of the book you'll be doing some preparatory work to make sure that all the great knowledge you have will translate into the right kind of business for you.

We'll talk business models, ideal customers and what kind of life style you want to achieve from your business. I'm sure you agree that it's hard to create a map or strategy, unless we've decided what we actually want and how we want to get there.

You'll fly through this and might even come back to it later to refine some of your plans as we explore more about your options and opportunities.

Your Ideal Business Model

This is one of the most important aspects that you should consider when you want to start a business. If you don't define upfront what you'd like your business to look like and how it will suit your needs and purposes, the business will end up owning you rather than you owning it.

The sad truth is that most businesses do not follow a strategy of any kind. They are simply a result of accidental decisions, responses to customer needs, fire fighting or the pressure of making ends meet. They are reactive instead of strategic.

At the end of the chapter you will have explored different business models and be able to choose which one is right for you. It's one of the first things that needs to be addressed before we can move forward. And it's the same thing we do with all our coaching clients.

What is a business model?

I simply mean how will this thing you call a business make money? What form of operations will be behind it. So there are a few questions that you need to ask yourself, which will determine what sort of business you will be running.

Now, it's not chiseled in stone, you can of course change things, but I would like you to make changes because you chose to, not because you have to.

By the way, I don't judge your answers, I'm fine with whatever business you want to create. It's important that'll it serve you and your lifestyle.

My own business model consisted for years of me working alone, being able to work from anywhere in the world and it suited me well. Today I have staff, an office and a very different model. It has changed what I can (and can't) do, how much I turnover and the profit margin.

I suggest for most new Expert businesses to sell their time for money - running a service based business. Before you call the support line and tell me I'm crazy, bear with me!

Brian Tracy, the famous American author, speaker and publisher has discovered that 90% of self-made millionaires in the United States actually STARTED their fortune by selling their time for money selling their services.

So I guess if it's alright for 90% of self-made millionaires, it'll be good enough for you and me. The reason I mention this is because in the wealth creation industry 'selling your time for money' is almost like a dirty word. It's not - believe me! It only IS a problem if it's the only way you're making money. Even good old Richard Branson sells his time for money! He recently spoke at an event in London and got paid for his time. (Ok - it was £250,000 for a couple of hours, but who's counting!)

So don't be afraid of selling your time for money, as long as it part of a strategy. As a matter of fact, 9 out of 10 of the clients I work with start that way and most keep an element of selling their services (the time for money aspect) - but at the right (read high) price.

'Services' is a broad term for selling your expertise that may include consultancy, coaching or a form of teaching or training. Coaches, teachers, trainers and public speakers regularly use this 'service-based' model with great success and although we don't want you to depend on it, it's often the fastest and easiest way get started.

If you prefer to develop and sell your own physical products like gadgets, then your road is very different. It'll be slower, less predictable and more expensive to get started. It includes challenges like manufacturing and distribution - often at low margins and can only work in high volume. For most individuals this is not the place to get started!

In essence there are only two basic ways to make a good amount of money. Selling loads of units at a low margin or selling small quantities at a high margin.

You need to decide which you prefer, but I have a clear favourite. The Expert Success business model is pretty much rooted in the service-based model. When we talk about 'products' in the Expert space, we normally mean 'published knowledge' - a high margin, low cost way of producing leverage for yourself.

One more important consideration is if you want to be in the limelight like me, being very present and 'out there' or do you prefer a more hands-off business where you sit in the background, and let your products do your talking?

Again, both is possible, but the standard Expert Success model clearly favors the first one.

Considerations for deciding your Customer Segment

One of the main distinctions that all of our coaching clients come to appreciate is the need to cater for a small, narrow but higher-value and more affluent demographic or market.

As I mentioned before, you can either be a mass market offering with high volumes and low margins, or decide to deliberately position yourself as being exclusive and expensive, thereby needing a much smaller and more affluent segment of the market. If I had to give you an example from the high street, in the chocolate market, you got to decide if you are 'Thornton's' or 'Hotel Chocolat!' And of course every country in the world and every market and industry has its own equivalent to this.

Yet when it comes to starting their own service based business, most individuals don't make this decision consciously to their detriment. This is an unavoidable decision you need to make. Decide right now who you'd like to work with and who you'd rather not work with. Decide that you want to work in the premium end of the market, with people that will happily pay more for the higher quality products and services!

Or let me ask you a clarifying question: Would you rather compete on price with everyone else trying to sell to people who don't have money to spend?

Here is my simple conclusion from having observed the challenges of small businesses and solo-preneurs:

> *Top Tip: "It's infinitely more difficult to be successful competing with businesses on high volumes and low prices, rather than charging premium prices to a smaller and much less price-conscious clientele."*

As a side benefit I can almost guarantee that you'll enjoy the working relationships you have with your clients a lot more. So make a conscious decision: position yourself as 'up-market', not 'mass-market' - it's hard to do both!

Design Your Future Lifestyle

Now that you have considered your business model, let's consider how this business model will work (or play) with the rest of your life - let's design your future lifestyle. All this means is what kind of life you want to lead. Weirdly enough, many people never even ask the question, but just accept whatever society expects of them. Here is the good news - you do have a choice in this matter.

One of the first questions you need to answer is what type of business you'd like to run in order to support your lifestyle? It's vital that your business serves you and your lifestyle preferences and not the other way round.

> *Top Tip: A business is defined as a profitable enterprise that works without you being there and it's there to support your chosen lifestyle*

Mmh, judging by this parameter, there are many people who are not running a business at all! But let's get back to the lifestyle question. How will your future business fit around your ideal life? Here are a few questions that will help you clarify this. Just go for what instinctively seems right for you. There is no right or wrong answer here, just make a decision.

Full-Time or Part-Time?

To start with, you need to decide how many hours you'd like to work in your business. It's important to be clear about whether you're looking to work full-time in your business or whether you want to eventually spend less time in it.

Just a word of warning (and apologies to Tim Ferriss): Forget 'The 4-Hour Workweek' fantasy. It will take a LOT of hours to get your business off the ground, even with all the cool stuff you are learning here! And I know that Tim is a workaholic, and worked like a maniac to get the success he enjoys.

But since Tim's best seller there has been a myth perpetuated around the Internet that you can make serious money without work and people have been chasing that illusive carrot forever – without success! Thinking they got the 'wrong system' or just missing some 'push button software'. Please! Do me a favor. Stop dreaming and come back to the real world...

So let me share some home truths with you, clear up some myths (which seems to be particularly persistent in the internet marketing industry) and share some wisdom from my experience in business and studying other peoples' businesses.

There is no consistently successful Expert business that works without you being there, especially at the outset. It is possible to create a highly leveraged, hands-off business, but the reality is very few ever achieve it, and this is something that you can do in a couple of years.

When you're first starting out it's very likely that you'll work full-time or even more than full-time. Everyone I know who is truly successful works hard and enjoys hard work. I don't mean digging up the road, but if you are being passionate about your business and your mission, you can't help but being active and excited about your work!

This doesn't mean spending hours and hours doing useless tasks but instead working strategically on their business. Later on you may choose to work part-time in your business, while your business is being managed on a full-time basis with some key staff running the operations, allowing you to pursue other activities to fulfill your life's purpose.

If you are a start-up or are in your fledgling years, it's 'all hands on deck' and be committed to get the ball rolling. When a business grows from a small, one-man-band to a small team in the next couple of years, then it will be organic growth and you'll know every task that your staff will have to do - because most likely you'll have done it yourself. This will by the way, make outsourcing of tasks or jobs a lot easier, as you know exactly what you want the outcome to be.

> *Top Tip: As much as you may aspire to make money without working, a better strategy is to find a business that you love to run. When that's true, much of your fulfillment in life and the purpose of your existence will come from actually running and helping to grow the business you're so passionate about.*

Your Take-Home Income

The next consideration when designing your future lifestyle is the take home income. It's surprising how many people have never thought about this or have simply chosen a random number. I recently attended a mastermind meeting with some property investors, where one lady told us she was only 12 properties away from her goal of owning 100. When I asked her why she had chosen that goal, she didn't have a business based answer, she just 'liked the number'.

Ask people how much they want to earn and they come back to you with random numbers like £10,000 a month or £100,000 a year or indeed the very much-quoted 'a million' which would supposedly make them millionaires.

The problem though is that most of those numbers are random. From my research they are based on nothing but an idea of how much they think will make them happy or how much they think they could achieve. Both of these concepts are of course flawed.

Other 'strategies' include comparing themselves to a person that they hold in high regard and aim for less than they earn or they compare themselves with a person that they feel superior to and believe they can outperform them!

Now that I have shared with you a few ways that make little or no sense, let me share a way that helped me and many of my students to get a handle on this question.

Here are the components to consider: How many products/ services do you have to sell? How much of your time will they take to be delivered that will delight your customers? How much will it cost to deliver these products/services (production, marketing, fulfillment,...)? Then you can quickly work out if your model is actually realistic!

Choosing Your 'Access Model'

One the most overlooked but important considerations that will determine your future lifestyle depends on what types of products and services you'll offer to your prospects. We'll talk a lot more about products and services in the 'Producing Powerful Products' section of this book, but it's important from the outset that you design a business that considers the amount of access you'd like your future clients to have to you directly. There are just three different access models:

- The Full Access Model

- The Mixed Access Model

- The No Access Model

An example of the 'Full Access' Model is in person, one-to-one coaching. The advantages of this level could include premium pricing while the drawbacks are scheduling lock-ins, travel restraints and associated costs and the lack of scalability.

A good example of a 'Mixed Access' Model would be group coaching by phone or webinar. This still supports premium pricing, has a higher return on your time and allows you to upsell further services. This model is also prone to the drawbacks of scheduling lock-ins and lack of scalability, but has higher leverage.

Over the next few pages we have listed a range of different products and services that fit into each of the three categories. The 'No Access' model has the largest amount of products and services you could create and sell.

When we do this exercise in our Expert Success Academy, I ask the students to choose at least two from each section that they do not already have in their product/service portfolio.

> *Top Tip: One of the 'No Access' models I've consistently profited from over the last six years are physically delivered products at low and mid-range price points. They are often 'home study courses' or 'DVD Sets' from events.*

No access low and mid price products allow me to reach a wider market with my message and brand, while at the same time are totally outsourced to my fulfillment house.

NOTE:

For your convenience I have put all the exercises into an easy to download and easy to print pdf file. It's better than writing in the book :-) just go to following url to download it: *http://ExpertSuccessBook.com/workbook*

EXERCISE: Decide Your Core Business Structure

What Kinds Of Things Do You Want To Do In Your Business?

The crazy thing about a lot of people's businesses is that they don't define in detail what they want to do ... and so they become reactive instead of strategic and go off in all sorts of directions. This lack of focus means missing big opportunities.

Without over-thinking it, what do you want to do in your business? What are the solutions people will be coming to you for? And what do your most enjoyable customers look like?

Write down what you can about your preferred products, services and customers - whatever you can come up with in 5 minutes. (Hey, if you're an overachiever you can spend more time on it! - but spend at least five minutes on it - it'll pay off!)

What kinds of things do you want to do in your business? (What solutions do you want to provide?)

_____

_____

_____

_____

_____

_____

_____

_____

What kinds of customers do you want to work with in your business?

_____

_____

_____

_____

_____

_____

_____

_____

_____

_____

What Kinds Of Things Do You NOT Want To Do In Your Business?

Another area of business that people tend to skip is what they want to exclude, or 'filter out' of their business model. It could be certain types of products or services. It could be a specific type of customer (or a personality type).

I always say: 'Saying NO to the wrong kind of business allows you to say YES to the right kind of business'.

Now I get that this can be hard when you're starting out. When I got started I worked with absolutely anyone who was willing to pay - looking back I wish I had said NO to a lot of that early business.

Without over-thinking it, what do you NOT want to do in your business? What are the solutions you don't want to offer that might be expected in your industry? Just write down what you can come up with in 5 minutes. (Overachiever? You can spend more time on it!)

What kinds of things (solutions) do you NOT want to offer in your business?

_____

_____

_____

_____

_____

_____

_____

_____

_____

_____

_____

_____

_____

_____

What kinds of customers do you want to AVOID working with in your business?

_____

_____

_____

_____

_____

_____

_____

_____

_____

_____

_____

_____

_____

Picking And Choosing Your Channels Of Income Generation (In different Access Models)

Think about these channels carefully and think about how you're going to want to scale your business as time goes by. Choose the ones you think would be ideal for your business structure. If you're not sure, use your gut instinct.

'Full Access' Income Generation Models

With this model, you're trading time for money - this can be very lucrative, but doesn't scale well.

Income Generation Mode	Advantages	Drawbacks
In-person (one on one)	Premium pricing	Scheduling Lock-In, Travel, Does not necessarily scale well
In-person (small group)	Premium pricing, higher ROI, upsell potential	Scheduling Lock-In, Travel, Does not necessarily scale well
Phone / video access	Premium pricing, visibility	Scheduling Lock-In, Does not necessarily scale well

'Mixed Access' Income Generation Models

With this model, you're giving less 'real time' access to you and leveraging your time investment.

Income Generation Mode	Advantages	Drawbacks
In-person (seminar)	Premium pricing, higher ROI, high visibility, upsell potential	Scheduling Lock-In / Travel
Group coaching (phone)	Premium pricing, higher ROI, upsell potential	Scheduling Lock-In
Group meetings (online)	Premium pricing, higher ROI, upsell potential	Scheduling Lock-In / Tech issues
Online forums (where you participate)	Flexible scheduling, strong selling point	Does not necessarily scale well, can consume lots of time
Email support (products or services)	Flexible scheduling, strong selling point	Does not necessarily scale well, can consume lots of time
Email coaching/ consulting	Flexible scheduling, strong selling point	Does not necessarily scale well, can consume lots of time
Client services requiring interaction (back-and-forth with the client)	Potential premium pricing	Unless clear boundaries exist, can become a time suck
Client services requiring only response (you give advice / critique on clients' situation)	Higher ROI	Potential for lower pricing

'No Access' Income Generation Models

With this model, you're getting maximum time ROI (in some cases in return for lower prices)

Income Generation Mode	Advantages	Drawbacks
Done for you' services (no interaction, e.g. blog setup)	Reach wider market, hands-off (can scale infinitely)	Without high traffic/list volume, revenue is limited
Digitally delivered products (low price point)	Reach wider market, hands-off (can scale infinitely), can be used as bonus material	Without high traffic/list volume, revenue is limited
Digitally delivered products (high price point)	Can be easier to sell, premium upsell opportunities later, more affiliate interest, can be used as bonus material	Takes more savvy to get into markets that can pay
Physically delivered products (low price point)	Reach wider market	Requires high traffic/list, costs to scale, profit margin lower
Physically delivered products (high price point)	Can be easier sell, premium upsell opportunities later	More expensive to produce, costs more to scale
Digital membership site (fixed payment)	Hands-off, can be premium priced, controlled environment for up-selling	
Digital subscription site (recurring payments)	Can be premium priced, controlled environment for up-selling	Constant content creation
Free online content (blog)	Excellent list-building tool, credibility builder, opens up affiliate opportunities	Constant content creation

Income Generation Mode	Advantages	Drawbacks
Online forums (no participation)	Hands-off	Requires high volume to work, Can die out if not tended to
Affiliate promotions (active 'pushes')	Extremely high time ROI if your audience is well-targeted	High-traffic blog or list needed, finesse needed to avoid 'burning out' your audience
Affiliate referrals (passive referring links)	Extremely high time ROI if your audience is well-targeted	High-traffic blog or list needed
Advertising	Essentially 'free money'	Can distract from your own sales message, unreliable cash flow, no brand leverage
Reselling (other people's products/ services)	High time ROI	Generally puts you on the hook for support; you're at the mercy of the vendor's quality control
White Label (Letting others repackage your product/service with their branding)	High time ROI	Does not build your brand

Choosing The Right Customer

Following on from your business model and future lifestyle, this is the third of the questions most people never ask themselves before getting started in business. From my experience though this is one of the most important ones. I had an epiphany when one of my friends in property shared with me the exact tenant profile he was gearing his offer towards. I realized that my business was no different. And neither is yours. So:

- Just who is your perfect customer?

- What do they want or need?

Let's consider these two very important questions in more detail. After all, these are the people that will pay for your future lifestyle and help you fulfill the purpose of your life :-)

Who are they?

When we talk about your future customers and who the right customers are, I use a simple strategy called profiling. I suggest that you profile your future customers into three categories that relate directly to the price range of products or services they will buy in the future.

The logic is simple; people who buy low price products will most likely be a different category to people who buy high price products. This doesn't necessarily mean that people who buy high price products exclusively buy high price, but high price product or service customers need to fit certain criteria.

It's important to identify people with mid range and high end spending power as this is where a majority of your profits in your business will come from.

When we define your 'product staircase' in the 'Products' section of this book, it'll become clear how important it is to have multiple products to sell.

The following exercise will help you complete the profile of your ideal future customers. A simple but effective tip that helped many of our coaching clients is to give your future customer a name. Imagine them as a real person, living in a real city, with a real job and having a real need. If you can clearly picture who your future client will be, it will be much easier for you to complete this profile exercise.

When creating your ideal customer in detail, you'll naturally start to define some polarization. This means not everybody will love you or your brand or products. Some might even hate you! And although that sounds distressing, let me comfort you that it will be important and necessary to have such a strong position in your market that you will create polarization.

> **Top Tip: To polarize opinion is very important if you want to develop a loyal following or tribe. As I always say in my presentations, 'You need to decide what you stand for and what you stand against'.**

EXERCISE:
Choose The Right Customer

Who are the customers that you want to sell your Products/Services to?

If you don't define (and segment) your customer, you're going to make a fraction of the sales you could be getting and you'll make your job a whole lot harder than it needs to be. Let's talk about your 'customer profiles' and what that means for your business.

You're going to think of the 'types' of people who want to buy what you're selling. The simplest way to do this worksheet is to think of a few actual people who are (or could be) customers and think about a general description for them. Copy the worksheets or print them out and complete one for every person you think of (customer avatar)

Characteristics	Description
Income level	
Age range	
Attitudes / personality Traits that define them	
Hangouts (Favorite blogs, websites)	
Polarization: Who they love / support / want to be like	
Polarization: Who they hate / avoid / don't want to be like	
What's important to them as people / as how they want to be seen	
What's important to them about how they want to do business	
Best strategies to get them interested in your message / offer	
What they will buy from you right now	

Characteristics	Description
What they will grow into needing to buy	
Why do these customers come to you as opposed to the competition?	
... or as opposed to doing nothing?	
What levels of access do these customers tend to want most?	☐ Full Access ☐ Mixed Access ☐ No Access
How much can they afford to spend in a given year?	£
What's your return on time/effort for this access (is it a good deal for you)?	☐ High return on my time ☐ Return on my time ☐ Low Return on my time
Are these customers high-maintenance or low? (Do you enjoy working with them?)	☐ High-Maintenance Pain ☐ Easy / Fun To Work With
Are they proven buyers or do they have high spending friction?	☐ Easy Sells Who 'Get It' ☐ Hard To Convince

Characteristics	Description
Do you see these customers moving to a higher tier / making more purchases?	☐ Yes, proven purchasers ☐ likely one–time buyers
Will these customers be the most profitable in the long run?	☐ (Pursue them!) ☐ (Avoid them!)

> *NOTE:*
>
> *For your convenience I have put all the exercises into an easy to download and easy to print pdf file. It's better than writing in the book :-) just go to following url to download it: http://ExpertSuccessBook.com/workbook*

Once you have a clear picture in your mind of who your future customers are, next it's time to work out just what they need to solve their problems, to answer their questions and to relieve the pain they are feeling in certain areas of their life.

I want you to discriminate between products and services and also discriminate between immediate needs and future needs. Some products will help people to immediately solve a problem whilst others are future purchases that are not relevant in their current situation but will become important at some stage in their future development.

What do they need and want?

There are two different types of products; digital information products and physical products. For instance, an example of a physical product would be the DVD set we produced following the 'Expert Success Summit' Event in September 2012. That's something somebody might well want to have on an immediate basis because they attended or heard about it and they wanted to get access to the information that was covered at that event.

From my experience, physical products command a higher price compared to purely digital information products and reduce refund rates. Whether you choose to produce physical or digital products is a choice you need to make, although of course you may want to do both.

Information products are often delivered in purely digital format via membership sites or as a set of downloadable files. I've created dozens of successful products in our product family, both digital and physical.

Another good example of a physical product is our monthly 'Expert Success' newsletter and audio CD, which are sent to all our Expert Success Academy members.

The 20 page monthly 'Expert Success' Physical Newsletter and Audio CD which is sent to all Expert Success Academy Members worldwide.

Immediate vs Future Needs

Another key distinction worth making is between your customers' immediate and future needs. In the example of the Expert Success Summit DVD set, their immediate need was to learn more about how to become an Expert in their chosen market and learning more about my company Expert Success. The 'Expert Success' Newsletter and

CD however is in most cases a subscription purchase our customers make after they've known me for a while.

From a business perspective, newsletter subscribers are a source of recurring income that is predictable and help with key business metrics such revenue and profit forecasts.

Let's look at services now: similar to products, I divide them into immediate and future needs. Some of the services your customer will require and consume immediately, could be a live training event. The demand and desire for live training events will - in my opinion - never go away no matter how sophisticated online communication tools become. People always value the amount of live support and interaction that takes place during a live event and it is the most powerful way to create trust and connection which is perfect to ascend people through your product and service staircase.

One of those live training events is our 'Online Brand Masterclass', which we run regularly in the UK and as a differentiator to most courses includes a 'Done-For-You Service' element. I'd strongly encourage you to think if there's any element of your future business where you could offer a Done-For-You Service. This will allow you to charge higher prices, guarantee outcomes and create long term customers through service based continuity like follow up coaching or hosting and support packages.

These services will increase what is known as the 'stick rate' (how long your client continues to purchase your services) due to the high 'pain of disconnect' (how easy it is for people to stop using your services).

One of my preferred services that can serve an immediate and future need for your customers is coaching. I would encourage you to see if there is a coaching element to your business you could extend or offer. Our coaching programs provide multiple levels of coaching including Gold, Platinum and Diamond and Mastermind. In exceptions we also offer and deliver bespoke programs. These are normally offered only to long standing clients and I would urge you to make those the exception rather than the rule. At the end of this chapter you'll find a matrix of all our coaching levels that might serve as a useful model for your own business.

When you design your future business and create products and services for sale, make sure there are at least a few products and services that people can continue to consume either in the form of recurring products, membership sites or higher level aspirational products and services. For example, in my business, we offer further live trainings to deepen and extend your knowledge about the importance of a high-quality, personal online brand, expert positioning, product creation and cultivating a buying audience. All are clearly linked to Expert Success.

Our range of Done-For-You services leverage our in-house team and outsource specialists and allow us to offer specialist high-end consulting and coaching services like product launch consultancy. These services need a deep understanding of the industry and a solid relationship with our clients.

Personally I can only vouch for the necessity of being in an ongoing coaching relationship. I have had a business coach and personal coach for the last three years. It is without doubt one of the key reasons for my success.

If you don't have the results you feel you deserve or the results you want - get a coach! Get the best coach you can get your hands on and that you can afford. From my experience it should feel like a stretch to pay for your coach so that you really value the relationship - especially at the beginning.

Because I have experienced the benefit of continuous coaching in my business and life, I am advocating continuous coaching to all my students, be it in Gold, Platinum, Diamond or Mastermind level. We've found that many Gold students over time move into our Platinum Program, and Platinum students move into the Diamond level and then Diamond students become Mastermind members. This natural ascension is implied in the levels and permanently seeded and talked about in the Academy.

The Expert Success Academy

Level	Silver	Gold	Platinum	Diamond	Mastermind
Monthly Newsletter	✔	✔	✔	✔	✔
Monthly Audio CD	✔	✔	✔	✔	✔
Monthly Coaching Webinar	✗	✔	✔	✔	✔
Access to Membership Site & Archive	✗	✔	✔	✔	✔
Private Face Book Group	✗	✔	✔	✔	✔
Monthly Live Meeting London	✗	✗	✔	✔	✔
Minimum 30% Discount on all Courses	✗	✗	✔	✔	✔
Monthly Live Group Coaching	✗	✗	✗	✔	✔
Weekly Group Coaching Calls	✗	✗	✗	✔	✔
Monthly Mastermind Meeting	✗	✗	✗	✗	✔
Monthly 1:1 Calls	✗	✗	✗	✗	✔
2 Day Retreat	✗	✗	✗	✗	✔
Direct 999 Access	✗	✗	✗	✗	✔

My Expert Success Academy Coaching Levels in a simple Matrix (details subject to change). What is smart about a model like this is that you simply take some of the benefits away from the lower levels.

That means you are not designing four different programs, but allow different levels of access to one coaching offer.

You will naturally allow more access to your time or your team's time for higher levels, creating higher price points and more exclusivity.

1.2 Create Your Online Avatar

Your online avatar is what people can find out about you in the online world. That doesn't mean you have to 'tell all'. The great thing about your 'Online Avatar' is that you choose and control what you want people to know about you (at least on your personal branded site). So this is not something that should be left to chance or be based on what others say about you. It's all part of your Personal Online Brand, the big first step to your Expert Success.

I have found that many Experts and Celebrities have chosen to build Personal Brands, have consciously created their own Online Avatars to exploit the attention they attract and to manage their reputation. So if you want to be seen as an Expert or Celebrity, you got to do was is expected - have a Personal Online Brand.

Your Personal Blog

Let's define what I mean by your 'Personal Blog'. A personal blog is NOT your business website. If you currently have a business with its own website, products and services, then your personal blog will not replace the site. Your personal blog is a website that is dedicated to the individual who is the public face of that business. You may be the Managing Director, CEO or other recognizable profile of your business. Your own personal blog is where people can find out about YOU and your interests, which may include one or more businesses.

You should also link to your Social Media profiles, allowing people to follow you any way *they* want.

Links to my Social Media

Links to my Business Partner's Personal Brand

Personal Blog - Your HUB

Links to my Businesses

Links to my Products/Services

In this picture you can see how your personal blog relates to your other existing websites and business(es). From the personal blog there are links to social media, business partners, businesses and products and services.

Most people hide behind their company identity hoping that a big name will give them more credibility. My experience is pretty much the opposite! People trust people, especially in the micro business arena, so show your prospects and customers that you're a real person!

The last decade has seen an erosion in trust towards politicians, corporates, churches, banks, multi nationals - in short - any structured enterprise, so it is now more important than ever to show people who is behind the products and services on offer.

People want to know who you are and you can share your values, what inspires and motivates you and what you stand for and what you stand against. When you do this, you'll find likeminded people who share similar values or aspirations will warm to you, connect with you and start to follow you. This is how you start to build a 'tribe' or an 'audience', who are far more willing to investigate your products and services further.

If you are wondering about the technical platform of your personal blog, it will most likely be on the very popular WordPress platform. This will allow you or your team to update that personal blog with as little technical knowledge as you need to write an email.

I like to compare the purpose of your personal blog to the CV of the 20th century. The big difference is of course that this new CV is multimedia, available to everyone online and working for you 24/7! Personal blogs, your online CV and personal timeline are rapidly starting to replace the CV - including in the minds of prospective employers and customers. The standard CV will soon be a thing of the past, as these days people will 'Google' you to find out anything and everything they can about you.

Check this for yourself: when looking to find out more about someone, did you 'Google' them? So does everybody else!

I would strongly recommend that you control as much information about you as you can. My own blog, DanielWagner.com has been running since 2007 and has been working for me 24/7/365!

It has all the ingredients of a Personal Brand: Personal domain (DanielWagner.com), a custom graphical header, a professional picture, a strapline (or promise), and of course many ways to connect - from Social Media to optin form to your email list.

There's also an easy way to find out more about me via my 'About Me' page, as well as other information about my interests and businesses. There are multiple ways to 'follow' me using Social Media or simply via joining my database via an opt-in box.

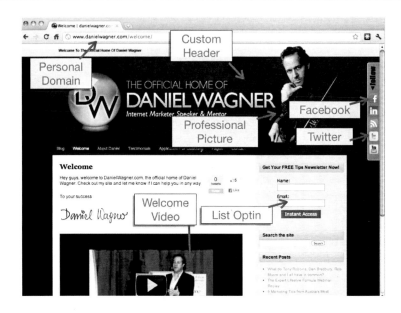

DanielWagner.com is a good example of a personal blog.

Many times people tell me that they are already on Facebook and LinkedIn, so why do I still recommend creating a personal blog? In today's world most people (and that is only ever going to increase!) will go online to find out more about you and you cannot leave it just to Facebook, YouTube, Twitter or LinkedIn to provide information about you and tell your story. It is also important to point out that these services change all the time and could delete or take down your profile at any time, which is a risk you don't want to take.

In my experience your Personal Brand is one of the best ways to showcase who you are, what you stand for, the businesses you're involved in and the values you hold.

Despite this massive opportunity to quickly and easily control your public image, which can have an immediate and lasting effect on our income and change your life, most people don't take any care about the appearance of their personal blog. Even worse - many people still don't have an online presence that represents them in the 'virtual world'. Trust me the impact of this 'virtual world' image of you are very, very real!

So here are some 'must dos' to make sure your personal blog stands out from the crowd and does the job it's meant to do. It's job is to share your promise, sing your praises, tell your story, build trust on autopilot and qualify prospects!

A Custom Banner

Only a few years ago you could impress people with just being online. Today it's a different story. WordPress and similar advances have made it very easy for almost anyone to have a decent looking website. So a professionally custom designed banner is one of the quick wins to make your personal blog stand out.

In my presentation on Personal Online Brand I share examples from James Caan, Robert Kiyosaki and of course, my own – to illustrate and highlight the commonalities.

Professional Photo

Your custom banner must include a professional photo of yourself, taken specifically for the purpose of your Personal Online Brand. I use John Cassidy, who specializes in head shots for web and social media. John has been doing all our and our students head shots and I highly recommend him.

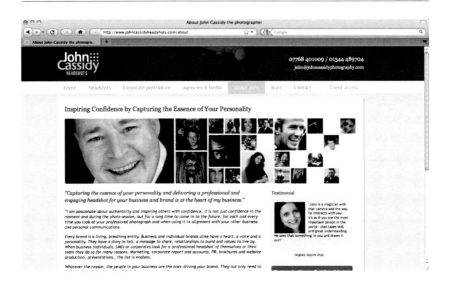

John Cassidy at http://johncassidyheadshots.com is my go-to guy for amazing looking portraits for your custom banner. If you get in touch with John tell him I sent you :-)

Your Name as a Domain Names

You should own your own name or a version of it as a domain.

The preferred suffix is .com, but you can also go for .net or .co.uk if you are working UK specific. Sometimes it helps to insert a hyphen (like http://James-Watson.com). You can check if your name is still available here: http://namecheap.com and buy it for around $10.

When I bought my name back in 2005 I actually paid $1,000 for it. You might find that someone has bought your name with the intention to selling it to. If that is the case and it's important enough for your business, (in my case I was clear that I would build a business around my personal brand) then you might want to make the investment depending on price asked. Always negotiate!

The very important Strapline

One of the most important elements of your professional custom designed banner is the strapline. In advertising this is often referred to as a 'slogan' - but I love BJ Cunningham's explanation that it constitutes 'your promise'.

People landing on your page should quickly and easily find out what you are about. Straplines should be kept short and pretty much tell people what you can do, how you will do it and sometimes even includes who you can do it for.

I have created over a hundred straplines for delegates of the Online Brand Masterclass and have worked on a 'Strapline Creator', which in essence guides you to your own strapline following four simple steps.

Here are the four steps:

1. Start with An Action Verb

2. Describe the Goal or Outcome

3. Mention the method of achieving it

4. Include the Target audience

Here are some great examples from Personal Brands we built over the last year. I always include the person. You will notice that within just one sentence you pretty much know everything you need to know about the person and if you are willing to investigate taking the next step…

Here are a just a few examples from recent delegates of our Online Brand Masterclass:

'Helping You Create Wealth With Commodity Trading'

'Creating A Laptop Lifestyle For Time And Money Freedom'

'Increasing Profits For SMEs Through Strategic Marketing'

'Creating Dream Lifestyles For Ambitious Mumpreneurs'

A second way to tackle the all important strapline - even simpler and still good enough - is to simply use a few words to describe what you do. Something like: Speaker - Coach - Mentor. Not as good as the four step process outlines above, but at least people know what it is you do.

A word of warning… don't confuse this with what corporate brands do for their straplines. Brands like Nike (just do it) have spend decades and billions getting their message into your head. That's not what we are trying to achieve here. We simply want to qualify prospects by telling them exactly what we can do for them and how we are going to do it. That's why I call it 'your promise'

The 'About Me' Page

The next 'must do' is the creation of your 'About You' page. This is probably the most important single page on your website because it is the first place a new visitor to your site will go to find out more about you.

'Coming soon', 'under construction' or 'this is an example WordPress page' (there is a reason why WordPress include the about me page in every installation by default!) doesn't cut it. In a way it's great for us that so many get it wrong, which means it'll be easy for you to stand out from the crowd.

On the 'About You' page people will want to find out more about you, your background and your history. They want to know why you're here and why you've suddenly turned up in their lives. I once heard Dan Kennedy explain that it's profoundly troubling for people when someone new enters their lives without a clear, easy-to-follow, background history that they can file alongside their mental image of you.

You will need to share an overview of who you are, your working background where relevant, personal interests and what your passions and goals are. You need to tell people explicitly what it is that motivates you and what inspires you to do what you do. Never leave people to 'work it out for themselves' because they rarely do. Instead, make it crystal clear who you are and how you can add value to others.

Liven it up with photographs and keep the paragraphs short. Make it interesting, create a journey. It's such an amazing opportunity to be able to tell people exactly what you want on this page. You can instill beliefs, trust, include humor – it's totally up to you, but understand that the power of this page is incredible. It will 'qualify' prospects for you 24/7/365! By the time people will contact you – they will be your kind of customer, because your story has 'filtered them out'.

Ideally you'll follow a story telling strategy or a story arc that we've all seen from many successful books and movies. Most of these stories follow a hero who goes through turmoil and challenges, eventually overcoming them only to face even greater challenges, before finally overcoming them to have a final breakthrough or epiphany that changes their lives forever. I sometimes refer to it as the 'Then, Now, How' story. That was then, this is now and this is how I achieved the success or the results that I have today. This allows people to clearly associate and align themselves with you.

Listen. Information alone won't help you succeed with online marketing. Why? Well, there is just far too much of it out there. So besides getting information, and knowing what to do with it, you need to make sure to get that information from a reliable source.

In other words...

Someone You Trust!

Me in the Austrian mountains. There is where I am from.

What I discovered was that many times when I would get on someone's email list, I'd end up unsubscribing simply because I didn't trust their information.... or them! To me, they were nothing more than a name on my computer screen trying to get my money. And I wasn't even sure it was their name! You know what I mean...

My story at http://danielwagner.com/about-daniel is doing a decent job telling people about my journey. By the time people contact the office, they know a lot about me and are often ready to 'do business'.

This will help to build a great connection and rapport which is fundamental to become a real leader in your industry. In today's world, people want to know who the person behind the business is, however small or large that business and they want to know what your 'mission' is. You need to tell them this if you want them to follow you. If you're not going anywhere, no one will follow you...

Just recently one of my clients said to me during our first meeting he already felt as if he knew me just from reading the 'About' page on my blog. Just think of all the rapport and trust building that had been achieved with this client before our first meeting – all done on autopilot.

Social Media Links

A third 'must do' for every personal blog is to include a range of social media links. It's best to keep that section small and simple by only including the most recognised social media links, such as Facebook, Twitter, LinkedIn and YouTube currently. This is a very fast changing market place, but essentially the few key social media platforms that are widely written about in the media and are most widely used should be enough unless you work in specific industries of narrow niche technologies.

The easier you make it for people to 'follow you', the quicker you can build an audience.

Opt-In Element

The final 'must do' and 'must have' element on your personal blog is what we call an opt-in element. I'll talk more about list-building in part three when we look at how to 'Cultivate a Buying Audience' but in short, an opt-in element allows someone who wants to follow you to join your email list and stay in contact with you. You will have seen this many times. They enter in their details, typically their name and their email address, are added to your email list software and will therefore be notified whenever you send out future updates or news about your business.

A slightly more advanced version of the opt-in element is to offer a 'Free Report' or 'Tips Sheet' that proves your expertise and authority in your market. You'll have seen opt-in forms that ask for your name and email address in return for a 'Free Report', e.g. my 'Top 7

Secrets', '7 Strategies', or 'Biggest Mistakes to Avoid' or similar. Although a very simple concept, it is very effective.

Social Media

Social Media. You will have heard all kinds of superlatives around the term Social Media. Fact is, Social Media made the web interactive and even more importantly, more transparent. It's a phenomenon that has really taken over the majority of the traffic on the internet. Places like Facebook get more traffic now than the Google search engine. Why? Well, people just love to hang out on Facebook, chat with their friends, play games and interact with other people in the Facebook community.

Originally, websites were very much like online brochures, meaning you could look at but not actually interact with them. Social media sites are websites where you can both view and interact. For example, you can add comments to pages, create your own content, update your 'status' and generally let people know what you're up to. That's really the essence of social media – being social and interacting with other users of the site.

We as human beings are - by our very nature - social creatures. We are curious about other people, we love to know what is going on in other people's lives and of course we love to stay in touch with our friends. Social Media sites allow you follow people and stay in touch, just as people have always done via traditional means such as via letters or via phone calls - just quicker, cooler and from every mobile device!

The internet has made the world a global village and not only is it easy to stay in touch wherever you are, it happens instantly and in most cases totally free of charge. This is why Social Media services have grown like wildfire.

From a personal branding point of view it's important to have a profile on at least the major social media networks such as Facebook, YouTube, Twitter and LinkedIn. You might choose alternatives or additions to these, but if you're new to social media and personal branding, then start with those four. If you're a video person and love presenting or recording videos then YouTube might be your first place. If you prefer sharing shorter updates to your life, then Twitter (a micro-blogging update tool which limits you to 140 characters per update) might be your preferred social network. If you want to update people in more detail then possibly Facebook would be your preferred hangout.

The reason why you want to have more than one Social Media link is that different people love different services. Different people want to 'follow' you in different ways. All these social media sites allow people to subscribe and follow you and then get updates whenever you choose to update your profile, your status or share a resource. This means that people get reminded about you, your products and services as well as what you're up to personally, which builds deeper connections. This massively increases the likelihood of developing prospects into future customers. LinkedIn, which has in the last few years seen tremendous growth, is a tool mainly used in business to business and helps you build a valuable network of business contacts.

Reputation Management

In today's world, one of the first things someone does if they want to find out more about you (long before they'll do business with you) is to head straight over to Google, type in your name and hit return. What will they find?

If you are not sure, then I can assume that you don't have a reputation management strategy in place.

You see, many of your future customers will go into private-detective mode scouring the Internet looking to find anything negative they'll use to justify why they should NOT pay any attention to you.

And that's not some fanciful theory either, it's the stone-cold reality of everyday life.

So, if people are going to Google you to see what they can unearth about you, then 'reputation management' is the process of you proactively ensuring that people will discover information, links and references in their Google search that you're happy with. The only way to do that is to contribute much of the information via your personal brand and social media yourself. You wouldn't let anybody write your CV, would you?

Let me give you an obvious example. You might have heard or read in the papers that employers these days regularly check Facebook to screen their prospective employees. They are looking why NOT to employ them! So be aware of this when you next share stuff on your public profile!

Reputation management in the corporate world and for larger celebrities is the job of a full-time 'Reputation Manager' but for minor celebrities like you and me it only takes a few simple steps to make sure that your reputation stays clean.

Now that you have been made aware, you just have to make sure that reputation management is just another part of what you do (or get done). Unlike your CV, you cannot control and change your online reputation in a Word document. Instead, your online reputation is a summary of all the information that is out there about you online, and it's up to you to keep an eye on it. And it's hard - sometimes impossible - to get rid of stuff once it's out there.

TopTip:

1. Monitor your social media. Keep an eye on Twitter and Facebook. Who includes you in conversations? Who tags you in conversations or pictures?

2. Set up a Google alert for your name, your products and your brand to follow conversations where they are mentioned. This is how you can see who's talking about you, see where in the world your name is mentioned and in what context. This allows you to reply and respond to information about you.

One word of advice though, don't let paranoia set in. If you behave ethically, have good products and services and look after your customers, the majority of information about you will be positive and will help you to build a future-proof personal online brand.

A final element for active reputation management is to share the success of your clients. These are people who've worked with you and are effectively endorsing you. If you can share the stories of their successes via your social media pages that is only going to serve to enhance your reputation and attract more like-minded people to become clients of yours.

1.3 Achieving 'Expert Status'

Brilliant news upfront: Expert Status is generally not awarded – it's just claimed! You need to go out there and let people know that you *are* the Expert. Put it on your business cards, stick it on your blog strapline. If you are still waiting for some authority to call you up and tell you you're an Expert, then you'll wait a long, long time.

I came across this powerful concept for the first time in Vanish Patel's Property Networking Club. I was a total newbie to property, business and marketing back in 2004 and Vanish ran regular meetings with around hundred people in London. But one thing that really stuck with me is that he pigeon-holed people into areas of their specific expertise. There was the 'Property Sourcing Expert', the 'Property Finance Expert', the 'Overseas Property Expert' - you get the idea. This specialization made it easy for people to know who to turn to for advice. In reality, many of these 'Experts' had skills in other areas as well, but labeling them this way was a very powerful and clever frame. I have used this approach ever since when helping people to decide on their 'Unique Positioning' in the market.

So in this chapter I'll tell you the steps you can take to quickly become a recognized Expert in your chosen industry.

Using Expert Positioning

It's essential (especially in today's economy) to be positioned as an Expert. You can generally demand more money, have more influence and more freedom than similarly skilled or similarly experienced people in your industry. You will also have a greater sense of purpose, as you're better equipped to reach bigger audiences to share the messages they are so passionate about.

Let's look at an example from the self-development market, let's look at Tony Robbins. He is no doubt a gifted individual who used the knowledge of NLP that was created by others and made it into a public phenomenon. His Expert positioning allows him to demand higher premiums, have more influence over people's lives and decisions, and gives him the freedom to do whatever he wants.

An example from the UK Hypnosis and NLP market is Paul McKenna. In many people's estimation a just-above-average hypnotist and NLP practitioner, he positioned himself through his publications and TV programs to be the foremost authority in the market. This allows him to get paid more, influence more people and achieve higher levels of freedom and choice in his life.

The more people you can influence, the more people you can affect in a positive way through your products and services, the more money you can make. And if you are sharing a message you are passionate about, then more sense of purpose and fulfillment will be a natural consequence.

What do I mean by Expert Positioning?

In every market or industry there are a few people that get all the attention and make all the money. These 'Experts' have in most cases assumed this position deliberately. In many cases their skill level or true expertise is not superior to those of hundreds of others in their market or industry. This 'Expert Positioning' is what other people attach to you. What's important about expert status however is that most people think it's granted to them, bestowed on them by others including existing experts.

The Expert Success Matrix™

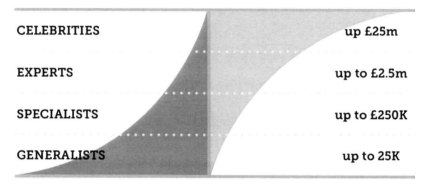

CELEBRITIES	up £25m
EXPERTS	up to £2.5m
SPECIALISTS	up to £250K
GENERALISTS	up to 25K

Your 'Expert Positioning' is based on the perception in the market place. But the perception has a very real impact on the amount of money you'll be able to make. Goal: do whatever you can to be higher up the matrix.

The surprising reality is that expert status is claimed rather than granted. You can claim to be an expert in anything that you choose to be. (I do assume that you actually have true expertise in your subject matter). The 'Expert Position' in any field can be claimed if you are willing and have the courage to stand up for yourself.

There are only a few simple conditions: You have to have a clear message (coming from your promise or strapline) about what it is you do and you must have a product or service that can actually change peoples' lives. Secondly you need to go out and tell people your message – again and again. All this will reinforce the perception that people have about you.

The word perception is key to this because in many ways it is your perceived expertise more than your true expertise that will define and influence your level of pay and your level of authority in your industry. When I present this topic from stage and share it with audiences, I use many examples to cement the simple truth that 'Perception = Reality'.

We'll talk more about 'tribes' and following later, but it is clear that most people like to follow. And they like to follow experts because everyone else does!

Using Your 'Then-Now-How' Story

The 'Then, Now, How' story is part of your way to build authority. Experts can demonstrate they've achieved knowledge and skill in a particular industry. It's crucial that experts can tell the story of the transformation that occurred during their journey.

In a recent interview I gave on this topic I describe it as follows: *'The transformation that occurred in my life has been an inspiration to many and is part of the reason why many people follow me, follow my journey and listen to my teachings. My life incidentally follows the classic 'hero's journey' story arc – the reluctant hero who overcomes struggle and adversity, is challenged again to overcome even greater adversity to finally – after a big 'show down' – achieves his dreams. Admitting and showing vulnerability, sharing human traits and not super powers, will make it very easy for people to connect with you and your story...'*

The example on my blog at http://danielwagner.com/about-daniel I mentioned earlier gives you a good idea of the format of a 'Then, Now, How' story. This includes talking about the past, the present as well as how you've overcome adversity in some way by solving a particular problem you faced.

Write your own 'Then, Now, How' story using the simple template that I've included in this section. Don't worry about being perfect, your 'Then, Now, How' story is always a work in progress and evolves as you journey towards your ever changing destination. But I would urge you to start today and to keep adding updates so that your online avatar stays up-to-date.

As you get more advanced, you might want to consider what emotion or belief you would like your readers or listeners to be in or have at the end of reading or hearing your story. For example if you want your readers to believe that they can achieve what you have achieved, then pick elements of your story that focuses on your self doubt that you could never ever achieve what you have.

So let's get started with your own 'Then Now How' story to create your Expert positioning.

> *TopTip: Expert Positioning is rarely granted, it is mainly 'claimed'!*

EXERCISE: Writing Your 'Then-Now-How' Story

Your 'Then-Now-How' Story should include at the least the following 4 elements:

1. Pictures or Video - to grab the readers' attention

2. Personal Story - to make a connection with your reader

3. Personal Problem and Solution - paint a picture of personal frustration or challenges and how you overcame the problem

4. Call to Action - Invitation to the reader to call you, fill in a form, send you a message, follow you on Twitter, like you on Facebook, subscribe to your blog

Opening Statement

_____

_____

_____

_____

_____

_____

_____

Background

_____

_____

_____

_____

_____

_____

_____

_____

Problem you were facing

_____

_____

_____

_____

_____

_____

_____

_____

Solution you came up with

_____

_____

_____

_____

_____

_____

_____

_____

_____

Call to action (call you, fill in a form, send you a message, follow you on Twitter, like you on Facebook, subscribe to your blog)

_____

_____

_____

_____

_____

_____

_____

_____

_____

Contact Details/Call to Action

_____

_____

_____

_____

_____

_____

_____

_____

> *NOTE:*
> *For your convenience I have put all the exercises into an easy to download and easy to print pdf file. It's better than writing in the book :-) just go to following url to download it: http://ExpertSuccessBook.com/workbook*

Publish Your Knowledge!

A key ingredient to Expert positioning is to publish your knowledge. Now you're reading my book now and without a doubt a book is one of the most effective positioning tools that ever existed. Especially in today's digital-overdose age, a book is the ultimate business card. Or let me be more specific: a well-written, well laid-out book is still the ultimate calling card.

As part of the Expert Success Academy we help many of our students publish their first book. This is why I thought it's helpful to create a little guide to writing your first book. I remember how daunting it is to sit down and start with a blank page!

The Book Writing Formula

How to Create Celebrity, Authority, Credibility & Believability for yourself

In your aim to become a recognized expert in your niche or market being a 'published' author is one of the guaranteed shortcuts.

The art and science of your 'positioning' is something that can easily be 'manipulated' (the dictionary tells me it means 'influencing a situation or person cleverly').

I want to share one of the best ways to boost the value of your offer I know of that helps your positioning in multiple ways.

Let me ask you a few questions:

Q: What do most celebrities have in common at least once in their lives?

Q: What do authority figures and authoritative experts have in common?

Q: What media tool lends itself to best create credibility?

Q: Which media is the least viewed as advertising and trusted as most believable?

So let's just quickly define celebrity, authority, credibility and believability.

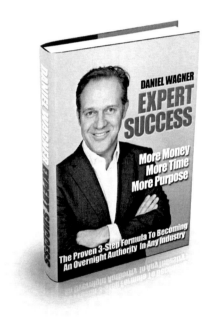

Celebrity - the state of being well known as an important person with stature and prestige.

Authority - power to influence others.

Credibility - the quality of being trusted.

Believability - the quality of being convincing.

No matter what you do right now, you do have a level of all these four qualities - but maybe not at the level you want or need to be the 'go-to-guy' in your field.

The Simple '9 Step Formula' For Writing your Own Book

1. Design the cover

What? First? Yes. I found it's a great way to help you get the book done. The Expert Success cover was designed before I went to work. It will most likely change (the Expert Success book was called Expert Success Formula and the Expert Revolution for some time!), but it sure helped me to get going.

Find graphic guys on elance.com and ask for book designers specifically. Get a 3d version done, print it out, stick it next to your monitor or on your whiteboard or fridge where you can see the thing - the visual will help you to manifest it.

2. 'Framework' It

If you want to write your own book, I would suggest you start by working out your 'framework'. The framework is the steps of your teaching method, your recipe for success. If you don't have a framework yet, just reverse engineer your successes. Look at your best clients or success stories and work out what you've done that made them succeed. Then break the work you've done down into logical steps and then find a good name for it.

In have created a 'framework name creator' that might help you with naming your framework. Have fun, keep it simple (below 7 steps) and then include a word like 'blueprint', 'formula', 'system' or something similar, suggesting an actionable path for your readers and future clients.

Ok, now that you have your own 'success formula' worked out, it's time to…

3. Mindmap It

Mindmaps are a great way to organize your thoughts or data and I recommend you use this tool to map out some more details of your book. Mindmaps are supposedly the way your brain organizes information. I found it's a great way to get complex information broken down into chunks. So far - every single person I asked to use them to structure their books have found the tool very valuable. You can simply use a big sheet of paper, but there are many software packages that are free or low cost for Mac and PC, even for iPads and iPhones, so take your pick. Just google mindmap software.

4. Record It

Not a must, but I have found that writers block can easily be overcome if you don't have to write in the first place! I found that a blank white page can be quite intimidating - so just record your thoughts following your structure of the mindmap. Every PC or Mac has built in software to record stuff. If you don't have a headset already, get a headset (a cheap one will do) and start recording. If it helps, do it with a friend or business partner and make it more interview style. You'll be amazed how much you know about your subject and how easy it is to create content.

5. Transcribe It

I don't suggest you do this yourself. Just go and outsource it. Go to http://elance.com or http://peopleperhour.com and find a person who loves to do that sort of thing. Within a couple of days you should have your first draft back. Now let's be clear. That will not be your book, but it's great to have some text fast to get started with.

You can also use transcription software that automatically converts speech into text. I had mixed results with this method, which could simply be because of my Austrian accent, but I in most cases it's not worth investing in software for this task.

6. Edit It

Now this is a job YOU should do. You want to make sure it's written in your voice but you can of course outsource this as well. I found that this piece can take a few days (or weeks!). Don't be too precious about it, but make sure it's done to a good standard - you are the judge.

Because you already have a good amount of transcripts done, what I suggest is that you read a paragraph at a time and then re-write it in a better version if necessary.

7. Set The Layout

Make sure it looks nice. Unless you are a graphic designer, leave this to the experts! Top tip - pick a book you love and have someone copy the style. Check out the outsourcing sites like http://elance.com and http://peopleperhour.com to get this piece done.

8. Proof-Read It

It's best to let someone else proof-read it. You are too close to the subject matter. Ask a few people - not just friends - and take the feedback on board. This step can drag on a bit, and I have seen people get discouraged at this stage. I also found that some people get a bit too precious about content and afraid to commit to a final version. I get it - it's never perfect

But it's more important your content and knowledge gets out there. There are far too many books that never see the light of day because the 'author' got cold feet. If you don't want to ask friends or colleagues, I have found a website that can help you get this job done. Just go to http://proofreadingpal.com.

9. Publish It

Ok. Don't wait to get published. That won't happen to most of us with your first book. So just go the simple route. When I share with people how easy it is to publish your own book, they are absolutely amazed and blown away! I normally recommend and use Amazon. They have a great service called at http://createspace.com. It's amazingly simple! Just follow the steps. If you need help, they have a great support service and if you want they have a lot of done-for-you pieces including layout and cover design services to pick from.

So there you have it. 9 steps to get your valuable knowledge out there in form of a book. But it doesn't have to be a book. I suggest to look at other ways to publish your content as well. This is not to replace the book strategy, but to supplement it.

Other Ways To Publish your information and content

Pretty much all published content will establish you as an authority. The word 'author' is included in the word 'authority' and this is certainly no accident. There are many different media that allow you to publish your knowledge and demonstrate your expertise. The following is not an exhaustive list by any means but gives you some options.

Articles

Articles are short, several hundred-word summaries describing specific areas of your knowledge or expertise. You can publish for free to sites such as http://Ezinearticles.com. People that regularly publish articles on Ezine Articles become 'Experts' in their market and are publicly acknowledged as such within the site. As a side effect, article directories give you good quality back links, which can help the SEO of your pages.

If you have written a book, you can use parts of it as articles, repurposing the content.

Reports

Longer than articles, reports are typically between 1,000-5,000 words. These reports are easier to write than fully-fledged books, but they can still provide very valuable information to your prospect market. They are also known as white papers in the corporate world. These reports can be market commentaries, they can be summaries of your knowledge, outlining your framework and your strategy.

They are great give-aways on your website and allow people to sample your knowledge. Again, if you have a book, this might be the first chapter of your book.

Newsletters

One of my favourite media for publishing knowledge is a newsletter. It's a vastly underrated media because newsletters don't usually have the glamour of magazines or other high profile media. However it's for this very reason that they are one of the most powerful publishing media. Newsletters are widely published in many different markets. There are free and paid newsletters, and newsletters that are published both online and offline.

One such example is our 'Expert Success' newsletter that is published for Expert Success Academy members. It's a monthly newsletter in both digital and print editions. Each edition is packed with articles, advice, editorial and tips for business owners and professionals looking to improve their marketing and become well-paid experts. It always includes success stories and offers. We even give binders to our members to collect them.

Blogs

Blogs are a great medium for publishing content to share with your online followers and your tribe. You can publish articles, tips and reviews etc, all of which helps you to build authority in your industry. Some people have built their whole business around a single, high-authority blog.

Interviews

If the written word is not your favourite medium, then interviews are a godsend. I've produced many interviews in my career online and some of the best content (and products) I've ever published have come from interviewing other Experts or being interviewed myself as an Expert.

With interviews, either you're the Expert being interviewed, or you interview the expert. Either way you get the credibility and it is the literal 'standing on the shoulders of giants', where their status or celebrity will be associated with you.

One of my first information marketing products published in 2005 was a collection of interviews with successful property investors asking them about their success habits. Not only did those interviews give me my first online payday, but it also established many strategic relationships that last to this day.

Podcasts

Another way of publishing your knowledge are podcasts. You can publish all your interviews via iTunes to peoples' mp3 players. Parmdeep Vadesha has used this strategy for many years and has created a very valuable following for his expertise in the property market.

They're easy and free to produce and another channel to publish your content and information that will widen your reach.

Online Video

In the past few years video has started to dominate publishing on the web, with YouTube being the most widely know proponent. Web TV today is a very viable alternative to any other form of publishing that allows you to run your own 'TV channel'. As television sets and computers converge, and with more 'Smart TVs' being permanently online, web TV allows anyone to have their own TV station and have their own following. This is a place that is sure to experience massive growth over the coming years. Watch this space for 'Expert Success TV'.

Live Performances

'Publishing' your knowledge can include live or recorded performances. This is something I've found to be very lucrative and very enjoyable, not only for my expert positioning, but also as way of building joint venture relationships and strategic partners. If you run events and training courses and get invited to speak on stage there is a natural assumption in the audiences mind that you are immediately an expert. We'll talk a bit more about this in 'Cultivate A Buying Audience'.

Instant Authority

Another strategy that can quickly cement your Expert positioning is called 'Earn The Right'. This is sometimes referred to as the 'elevator' pitch or the 'perfect pitch'.

In essence it quickly establishes your authority or proof that you can indeed do what you are claiming. Let's talk about the 'Earn the Right' Formula, its structure, how you can use it, and a short exercise for you to create your very own.

You can use this in your introduction, your home page, at networking meetings and literally anywhere you have to establish your credibility.

My 'Earn-The-Right' formula includes five elements:

Who are you?

How long have you been doing this?

How many people did you help/work with?

What results were you able to achieve for them?

Would they know someone who could be interested?

Who are you?

The first part is pretty simple. State your name or business name or market/niche you are working in. I suggest you use phrases like 'creator of', 'founder of', 'author of' to help build instant credibility.

This is a great place to use your 'strapline' or the 'promise' you created earlier.

How long have you been doing this?

The second element establishes how long you've been doing something, thereby giving you more credibility. (If you just got started, you can use my 'Borrowed Proof Formula' explained later in this chapter).

How many people did you help?

The next element is how many people you were able to help. This can simply be a number of clients, customers or businesses. There are couple of tips I can give you to make this more credible. If you worked with 30 something people, 'dozens' might sound more impressive. If you have only recently experienced growth in your business, you could say 'in the last twelve months alone...'. Generally it's a good idea to be very specific in your numbers.

What results were you able to achieve for them?

The next component I refer to as the 'A to B' element which means what level of success, improvement, or transformation were you able to achieve for your clients. Have you helped people make money online or increase their business profits? Have you improved people's relationships? Have you helped improved their health?

Here is a simple example for our friend John Smith, a marketing coach. As outlined earlier we have five simple components:

- Who is he and what does he do?
- How long has he been doing this?
- How many people has he helped?
- How much has he helped them achieve?
- Ask a question or use a 'Call-To-Action'

If we include the introduction and the call to action at the end, that gives you a great 'Earn-the-Right'.

Here is an example:

Here is his 'introduction and his promise', using author, founder and creator.

'Hi, my name's John Smith, author of 'Internet Profits', creator of the 'Internet Lifestyle Formula' and founder of the 'internet Lifestyle Academy' - I help people start their own online businesses and escape the 9-5 through digital marketing'

Here is his 'how long and how many'.

'For the last four years I've helped over 600 individuals and small businesses'.

Here is his 'how much has he helped'. This is clear demonstration of results, moving people from A to B.

'I've helped over 600 individuals and small businesses build their businesses by creating anything from a few hundred extra a month to multimillion dollar membership sites. I can show anyone exactly how to increase traffic, explode their conversion, and multiply their profits in simple and easy to follow steps using my 3 step formula'.

I use the 'which means that' idea to force you to talk about 'intangible' benefits of your results:

'Which means that they can now spend more time with their loved ones, have more financial security and finally live the life they deserve'.

Lastly you end with a call to action.

'Fill in the form on this site and I will send you my seven eternal laws of marketing to your inbox right away'.

Or if you were in a conversation, you might use a third party question not to be too direct.

'Would you happen to know of anyone who could benefit from results I mentioned earlier?'

By asking if they know anybody it detracts them from themselves and doesn't make it a direct question. However most people think of themselves first.

OK, now its time for you to create your very own 'Earn-the-Right'.

EXERCISE: Creating Your 'Earn The Right' Story

Before you get started, there are 5 simple elements to your 'E-T-R' - write them down, practice them and you'll see how natural it'll sound, even though you have followed a formula.

Your introductions will have more impact - no matter if in person or on video or on stage, the 'Earn The Right' is a big part of your 'Expert Tool Kit'.

1. Introduction and Promise

2. How Long

3. How Many/Much

4. Results A > B

5. Question/Call To Action

Introduction and Promise

_____

_____

_____

_____

_____

_____

How Long

_____

_____

_____

_____

How Many/How Much

_____

_____

_____

_____

_____

_____

Results (A > B)

_____

_____

_____

_____

_____

_____

_____

Which means that (explain intangible benefits)

_____

_____

_____

_____

_____

_____

_____

_____

Question / Call To Action

_____

_____

_____

_____

_____

_____

Memorize this and try it out next time you meet someone who asks you curiously: 'So what is it you do?' You'll be blown away what an impact it will make!

Unique Positioning

Unique positioning is one of the most important parts to be able to claim your Expert status. In this chapter I'll touch on why unique positioning is important and how to achieve it by following some simple strategies. I'll also look at who are the different audiences you need to communicate your unique positioning with.

Why You Need Unique Positioning

In an ever-more crowded marketplace, simply 'being an Expert' may soon no longer be enough to be wildly successful. It's therefore important to define and occupy your niche or 'micro niche' by having a genuinely unique offer or angle to stand out and have long term success.

The moment you decide what your unique position in your industry is, you'll have a clear competitive advantage. We'll talk later in the Product Creation part of this book on how to create 'packages' to avoid being price shopped, but it all starts with your unique angle in your market. People will take note and you'll naturally start to develop a following.

The Marmite Effect (Polarisation)

Once you take a position that people can identify with, both for and against, you've effectively achieved what I call the 'Marmite effect'. Yes, that means people either love or hate what you do.

Now, that doesn't sound very nice or desirable, but I guarantee you this is really important. Most people want to be liked by everyone and think they need to please everybody out there in the world.

Because you serve everybody, you goal is to appeal to people who are a close match for your ideal customer, i.e. they share your values and goals and your way of going after those goals.

What's important to notice about polarization and unique positioning is that unless you embrace the concepts you are doomed to being a 'commodity' - which means you will be bought on price!

Case Study - Domain Registrar

Let's choose an example that many people know online, GoDaddy. GoDaddy is the largest domain registrar on the internet. They happen to be a great example of the Marmite effect as well, which is also known as polarization.

Polarization occurs when you make a stand about something, and GoDaddy have a very deliberate view, which is embodied by their CEO, Bob Parsons.

In their marketing, GoDaddy like to use scantily dressed female models, especially in risqué TV commercials that typically get a lot of publicity, e.g. during the SuperBowl half-time breaks in the U.S.

The GoDaddy.com SuperBowl ads always polarize audiences.
But their target audience love them!

Now, obviously that's not going to appeal to women or to female audiences who could be offended by that kind of imagery. But do GoDaddy care? No, because that is the same philosophy of their ideal client. Now you don't necessarily need to take a stand that is political by any means, but you do need to stand for something.

Who will hate your Marketing?

If you find it hard to work out who will love you, try it the other way... Create marketing material that people will totally hate and work out who would hate it. Think about who would rip up your marketing material, steam in anger and be furious about what you have written and what you stand for! Now that's polarization!

And if you have someone passionate about hating you, there will be others who are passionately loving you. You will then have naturally created compelling material for their polar opposites!

> *TopTip: Trying to please everyone is the only guaranteed road to disaster, and the ultimate sin in Expert positioning and personal branding.*

How values influence Your Unique Positioning

The first question you need to answer is about your values. What do you stand for and what do you stand against? You might never have consciously sat down to work this out. But it's worth doing. Be clear and write them down. Create a vision statement (where you want to get to) and mission statement (how you intend to get there) and let people on your website know, include it in your marketing materials and in the interviews that people conduct with you and your clients.

At Expert Success we have our own 'values document', that has turned into our 'vision and mission' document. It's pretty simple and started out as a discussion about what we stand for and we believe the business is about.

Once you created your own document, there are just a couple of simple rules: everyone in your team or company has to know about and has to buy into the core values. And you never go against any and always honor at least one of the values in everything you do.

EXPERT SUCCESS VALUES

EXPERTISE - Quality, knowledge, applied wisdom

CLARITY - Simplicity, trust, honesty, integrity, transparency, being who we really are

FOCUS - Concentration, commitment, completion

LOVE - The absence of fear, treating others the way we want to be treated

RESPONSIBILITY - leadership, command not control, intuition, self trust

FREEDOM - Fun, not too serious, work is our play, pride

This was the first draft of out values document which we composed in a branding and team meeting early in 2012

Polarisation Case Study

I always share the brilliant example from the computer industry. For many years, Apple have run a polarization campaign with 'Mac' and 'PC' played by two actors. I call it the 'antagonist strategy'. It was easy for Apple to say what they stand for and who their target audience was. Both parts define their unique positioning - and just to mention: Apple is *not* being bought on price - but on the promise!

The 'I'm a Mac' and 'I'm a PC' campaign from 2006 ran for 3 years. The UK version of the campaign used the comedians David Mitchell and Robert Webb.

The 'I'm a Mac' and 'I'm a PC' campaign illustrated in a great way how we associate a personality with a brand. Corporates are spending millions on making their brands a 'personality'. This is where one of the key advantages of using the 'personal branding strategy' becomes apparent. You are already unique, just define your message, your market and keep sharing your story. People will naturally be attracted to who you are and the values you communicate.

Don't you think it's fascinating how close the 'Mac' and 'PC' founders are close to their brand avatars and target audience? This illustrates that a great brand is not just portraying an image to the outside world, but that the external image is a reflection of who they really are.

'I'm a Mac' and 'I'm a PC'. An early photo of Apple's Steve Jobs and Microsoft's Bill Gates.

> **TopTip:** *When who you are in line and congruent with your external image, a brand becomes naturally magnetic and aspirational.*

Let's leave the dizzy heights of Silicon Valley behind and look at some local small business niche examples. One of my coaching clients, Anthony Chadwick, founder of http://TheWebinarVet.com, who is 'Making Veterinary CPD easy' - positions himself alongside the independents and on a 'battle' against the corporate takeovers.

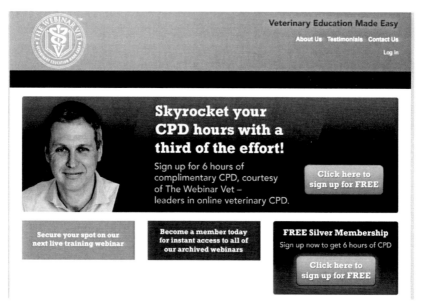

Anthony Chadwick's 'Webinar Vet Website'. Worldwide reach, multiple membership levels, and a very profitable business. The former practice owner is a prime example of unique positioning in a affluent vertical market.

Finding Your Own Unique Positioning and Market

When you create your own unique positioning, be creative, choose strong emotions and aim for clear positioning. Check with your clients and friends and 'test' your proposition. And remember the 'Marmite Effect'. You want to be anything but lukewarm.

If you feel you are in a 'crowded' niche or just a 'me-too' offer, then here is a trick I have used many times with great success:

Make your offer unique by either combining experience and skills (previous jobs, qualifications) or simply micro-niche to a market to become special.

I recently worked with a 'Property Expert', whose goal is to help people achieve financial freedom through property investing. (Real Estate for US readers). Problem is he wasn't that super qualified and it's a crowded market! So I dug around and found that he was a recruiting sergeant in the army!

So we micro niched his expertise to hep members of the armed forces create financial freedom through property. That is unique and I promise you that if you are in the armed forces he will be the only guy you'll ever work with because of shared values!

Who You Need To Position Yourself With

1. Your Followers and Readers

The first group is your fans, your readers and your prospective customers. Remember that you're the leader and they want to follow you.

People are looking for guidance and you have decided to step up and lead. They want someone they can believe in, who will help them in their decision-making. They want someone who can make them feel safe and happy, smart and healthy, or whatever it is that your services and products help them achieve.

Here are some golden rules to help you establish the right relationship:

- Assume they like you and want to do nice things for you.

- Make a habit of telling them what to do. That's why they decided to follow you.

- Give them consistent calls to action. Reward them when they do so and tell them repeatedly what you stand for.

- Find out what they want so you can give it to them. Ask them through surveys and other tools.

- Build profiles of your ideal fans so that you can connect with them better.

- Always be respectful and helpful. People do remember random acts of kindness.

- Use the strategy of unannounced bonuses for customers or prospects. People love to receive more than they bargained for.

2. Your Peers & Colleagues

The second group that you need to establish unique positioning with is your peers and colleagues. Get involved in their communities, there are always places to hang out together such as events, workshops or loosely arranged mastermind groups.

Maximize your impact

To maximize your impact with pace, send occasional traffic to your peers just as a gesture, but make sure they know where it came from! Encourage reciprocation by doing nice things. A line I love to use when people thank me is, 'I know you would do the same for me' (one of my favourite strategies from Dr Robert Cialdini's book 'Influence').

Buy yourself a new Peer Group

I'm always amazed that people don't jump on the opportunity to buy themselves a place in a peer group. I've done this many times in my life. I've always made my investment back many times over, and not just in monetary terms.

Build stronger ties than others

Most people are lazy and it's actually quite easy to stand out merely by doing a few simple activities regularly. Don't be one of the lazy ones.

I found it useful to also use channels outside social media to connect. Again, do what is unusual. Live events and conferences worked especially well for me. I personally prefer private connection phone calls or face-to-face meet ups.

Sometimes I even meet their family and become their friend. Be real and truthful - don't mess with this stuff. These are relationships which are part of your life - not just business.

Use unexpected media like postcards, letters and articles etc. I often buy little things as gifts (books are great for this and it doesn't have to be your own book) when I meet my peers. It's the thought more than the value that matters because they could buy their own stuff.

I have made hundreds of thousands of extra income just from looking after a few relationships over the years.

3. Gurus & Industry Leaders

A very important third group that you want to build a unique positioning and unique relationship with is your gurus, leaders or 'higher ups'. Now, with these people you might have to prove yourself.

Remember they're just regular people who are a few months or years further down the line than you, so don't be too star struck - but make sure you don't demand too much of their time or attention.

What NOT to do

Do not suck up to them because they will not respect that. Do not tell them 'oh my gosh your stuff is so great, you're so amazing'. It's good to show admiration and respect but do not subjugate yourself - they get too much of that anyway and no one likes empty flattery. Remember, you're good at what you do too and you can add value to them.

What to do

When you ask them for anything, be specific, make sure it adds value, and ask for small things first. This makes it easy for them to say yes to you.

A good strategy is to do your homework on your leaders, what they like, what they hate, what are their priorities. Try to find out what they tend to say yes to. Do they like interviews and if so what kinds of interviews do they usually agree to? Is there something you can do for them such as providing content for them?

You want to work with them, so what kind of people or topics do they like to involve themselves with? Look at their blog, buy some of their products, find out what they do and see how you can add value to their list and their business.

I was able to get the attention of some gurus and leaders by helping one of their successful students, some of their staff or some of the people they associate with without getting to them directly. You can expect it to take some time. You see, at their level of leaders and gurus, they ignore 99% of contact requests. Be patient and keep chipping away, its worth your while.

One of the simplest strategies I've found that works almost every time is asking 'what can I do for you' instead of requesting 'what can you do for me'. This sounds basic but you'll be surprised at how many people make this simple mistake!

> **TopTip: 'How can I help you sell more of your product' normally gets everyone's attention.**

Before I approach any guru or leader, I sample some of their products so I can make an informed decision about their status and authority before I even consider working with them. This also gives me numerous topics of conversation when I get the chance to speak to them.

Be creative. E.g. add their products to your list without taking affiliate commission or make some sales for them. That will get their attention. Call their office, become an affiliate, make them some money. That's a good strategy.

Just a word of advice. In case they don't want to work with you or ignore you - don't take it personally. You'll win some – you'll lose some. They have their own strategies and plans for the coming months and years, so if what you want doesn't fit into their plans there's a chance that they'll ignore you.

Social Proof

Social Proof creates Expert Positioning. I first came across the term 'Social Proof' when I read Robert Cialdini's book 'Influence – The Psychology of Persuasion' back in 2005. I have since read hundreds of marketing books, but I still regard Cialdini's 'Influence' as one of the best books on marketing - ever.

Cialdini's Influence is in my opinion one of the 'must reads' for every business man and marketer.

What I learnt about social proof is that 'what other people say about you is worth ten times more than what you say about yourself'. And of course this influences people's behaviour. It is widely used in business, in personal relationships and in marketing at every level.

Success Stories = Social Proof

So when a customer or prospect gives a testimony to the results that you were able to achieve for them through your teachings, products or services, you can use this to help other prospects overcome their fears, doubts or reservations. It also helps existing customers recommit to your company or service if they see other people recommit as well.

Nobody wants to make 'Mistakes' and look like a fool...

This is why Social Proof is so powerful - we look around for proof that the decision we are about to make is a good one. If we can see people like us (it is important that you can relate to the person giving the testimony) telling us that the decision they made was great and impacted their life and business in a positive way, we are more inclined to make the same decision.

Types of Social Proof Media

Audio and Video

The formula is always the same (shared later in the chapter), but you can and should use different media. Audio and visual social proof have become increasingly common as technology has allowed audio and video to be more easily created and consumed. I have found that pictures or videos with written excerpts work exceptionally well, as the picture or video creates trust and the written excerpt allows for a quick scan of the main benefit from the testimonial.

I've been told by numerous new clients that the video testimonials of my students really helped them make the decision to want to work with me. This is because, as mentioned before, what 'other people say about you is worth many times more than what you say about yourself'.

Emails and Letters

Although audio and video is great, do not disregard written media for social proof. You can get endorsements that are written from the clients or your peers. Emails or letters work very well, and I suggest you print them out and have them with you when you meet clients or show and read them when you present to an audience.

Unsolicited testimonials are extremely powerful and I always show a few in my presentations.

Proof of Earnings and Screen shots

You can also use proof of earnings with images from bank statements or merchant accounts. I like to show proof of earnings, but instead of just showing a screen shot, I log into my live merchant account and show live numbers - which is even more powerful.

The Book as Social Proof

Another form of social proof is to be the author of a book. Again that proves that you have enough Expert status to be involved in and be able to complete such a project. If you were an amazon best-seller on top of that – well – that would surely prove something!

Sold out events and Products

If your product is sold out, your event is overbooked and you have a waiting list for your service... that in itself is social proof. So if you have sold out, let people know.

Direct Social Proof

Direct social proof is from your students or clients; those who can testify to the results you've helped them achieve by working with you. Apart from testimonials for you as a person, your company may receive social proof from other businesses that specifically credit your company as having helped them move forward.

Even your products can receive endorsements. Having your products promoted by other individuals is implicit proof of the value that product holds. Joint venture partners, affiliates, people that promote your product are clear proof of the value of that product.

Make a habit of recording testimonials where you can and don't be shy to ask clients to give you testimonials.

Borrowed Social Proof for Your Products and Services

Here is an objection to my Social Proof strategy I get a lot:

'I don't have any examples of successful clients, I'm just getting started.'

If that is you, then it's time to celebrate, because I will reveal my secret 'borrowed social proof' strategy to you. Very few people know about this and even fewer use it.

There are two types of borrowed social proof you can use:

Borrowed Social Proof from People

First of all you can use social proof from other people – typically successful leaders in your industry or market. For example if you're an NLP coach or a Life Coach you might use Tony Robins as proof that coaching works. Tony Robins has helped thousands of people transform their lives with his coaching. Therefore coaching works, therefore my coaching works is the implied social proof. Your wording could look something like: *'Using the same strategies as Tony Robbins…'*

Borrowed Social Proof from Companies

The second category is companies. Again if you quote the success of companies in your market or niche you can borrow their proof.

A great example is in network marketing, where typically a new distributor has got no social proof of their own but they can use the success of the company they are working for as proof. So as a new distributor for Herbalife can cite the fact that *'the company you work with has launched hundreds of products and has got many tens of thousands of satisfied customers…'*

The 'Social Proof Formula'

Although testimonials are easy to record and social proof is easy to produce, most people waste hours of their time and produce ineffective testimonials. Almost any testimonial is better than no testimonial, but if you follow my 'Social Proof Formula', then you'll produce high impact testimonials every time.

If people want to testify that your products or service have helped transform their lives, then you simply must help them to give you a good-quality testimonial to help as many other people as you can to achieve the same results.

The 4 Step 'Social Proof Formula'

1. Before...

Before coming to the event or before buying a product or working with the person, I was... or I had...

Make sure you make them describe the problem with the 'before' state. Help them connect with the pain, use some detail and be specific if using numbers, places, dates.

2. Now...

The second component is 'Now I am...', 'Now I have...', 'Now I do...'

What has changed, what have they learnt from the product or service. Again, help them to be specific and use emotional language to connect with your readers, viewers, listeners.

3. Which Means...

Thirdly, what does it mean for their life or business, what is the direct benefit of the new learning or the new found knowledge?

What I love about step 3 is that it forces them to talk about intangible or indirect benefits, which people normally forget to mention.

4. That is Why...

A fourth addition is to encourage them to recommend you, your service or product so you can spread the word to others.

Now this is key – a clear call to action telling people what they should be doing next.

Example

Here's an example transcript from one of our students.

'BEFORE I worked with Daniel and James I had no clear strategy or marketing knowledge. I was just getting by.

NOW just after six months in the Expert Success Academy I have a clear vision of where my business is going, a fully mapped out product funnel and a clear strategy how to attract more clients.

WHICH MEANS that I can now fulfill the life of my dreams, spend more time with my family, and go on holiday whenever I want...

THAT IS WHY I would strongly recommend anyone who wants to create a better life and more profitable business working with Daniel and James if you have the opportunity to'.

EXERCISE: Your Perfect 'Social Proof' Testimonial

Here's a simple exercise that will serve you well. Pretend that you're your own best customer who has just been on a training course, bought your product and consumed your service. Therefore, you're absolutely delighted. Write a testimonial following the 4 step formula:

1. Before...

2. Now...

3. Which means...

4. That is why...

You can use that structure later on when you ask your clients to give social proof for your company business or service.

What people want are tangible results with a clear benefit to their lives and business!

If you could write your own perfect testimonial, what would it say? Imagine your perfect customer saying all the right things!

Before...

_____

_____

_____

_____

Now...

_____

_____

_____

_____

Which Means...

_____

_____

_____

_____

That is why…

_____

_____

2. Offer Multiple Products

As an Expert your products will largely be 'Information Products' or services like coaching and mentoring. Many service professionals only sell their time for money which creates two major problems. You run out of time and you leave money on the table.

To solve these problems we will talk about creating a series of strategically sequenced products and services, which are in large parts fulfilled automatically.

This way you can multiply your turnover, reach the biggest audience possible and work with highly qualified clients.

2.1 Map Your Product Staircase

Before I show you exactly how to design your own 'Product Staircase', let's start by defining exactly what I mean by a 'Product Staircase' and why it's essential you have one in place. Not only will a 'Product Staircase' help you achieve the business profits you desire, help you live the dream lifestyle you've always wanted, but it will also allow you to reach more customers and help them in more and better ways.

Definition of a 'Product Staircase':

'A product staircase is a range of strategically sequenced products or services that you offer for purchase at increasing price points. The purpose of these steps is to attract and develop your clients through different stages in their customer journey to maximize life time customer value and maximize your customers' results.'

Staircase Design

There are a few different variations of this concept, but in essence you start with giving away valuable information for free to build trust and establish proof of your authority. Based on the law of reciprocity you will dramatically increase the odds of your prospects becoming customers. At the same time you will pre-qualify your prospects without ever dealing with direct or personal rejection.

Your job is then to move people seamlessly from one step to another, from mid-ticket to high-ticket products (which can vary widely depending on your industry). You will have to learn to 'sell' people into the higher steps, but I have found that people naturally want to ascend if you have designed the staircase properly. We regularly have clients upgrade from one level to another based on their needs.

The FREE Line

The first product or products on your staircase are most likely free and will allow your new prospect to sample the quality of your information or knowledge at no risk. I call this the FREE Line and the more you can build trust with your future customers by giving them value, the better. This can included reports, white papers, videos, cheat sheets, quick start guides and so on. Ideally this is fully automated and takes none of your time.

The TRUST Transaction

The next step of your staircase is what I refer to as the 'Trust Transaction' - this is where money will change hands for the first time. I recommend this first step to be low ticket (around £20).

I encourage many of my students to offer their book at this stage, which has a proven price point and doesn't need explaining (like a membership site or bootcamp video series). A book has also the added benefit of being an authority piece in its own right, establishing your Expert status.

Another great trust transaction is a preview evening, discovery day or training day. You can charge £20-£97 for these sort of events and we've run all of these in London and in our offices for years now.

One of our 'Training Day' Events in London. We spent a whole day together learning how to build a £100K Expert business. Remember the chapter on 'Social Proof'? A sold out event and lots of happy people...

The MID Ticket Range

It makes sense to offer your new customers the logical next step. So make it logical! For example we offer a 3 Day Workshop called the 'Expert Success Accelerator' below the psychological £1,000 price point. I recommend to make this step a scalable group workshop. Naturally only a fraction of your attendees will take this next step. We'll look at conversion numbers and staircase economics later in this chapter.

HIGH Ticket Products

It's important to always offer a next step, because some of your clients will want to move further with you. They want more of your knowledge, time and attention, and it's only fair and makes business sense to offer them the higher level at a higher investment.

I recommend to offer fixed term coaching programs like the 'Expert Success Academy'. The Academy is a multi-level coaching model which lets people ascend and they are clear about the steps of the ascension from the outset. Proven and tested price points for programs like this are anywhere from £2,000 to £20,000 a year.

Some of my highest level products and services, like the Expert Success Inner Circle Mastermind – is an application only program, making it very exclusive.

Staircase economics

One of the main benefits of having a product staircase is simply economics. The majority of your business profits will derive from sales of your mid and high ticket products and services. This means that by developing your customers, offering them higher price points, your business profits will soar. This is an absolutely 'fundamental' law of building an Expert business that most business owners are simply unaware of or fail to implement.

One of the fascinating human aspects of offering a staircase or ascension model is that some of your customers just want to be in the top program, no matter what. They will always want to be in the 'Inner Circle', the 'Boardroom' or 'Mastermind Group'. So it is absolutely mandatory for you to provide this, so that different customers can buy what they desire!

TopTip: Create an ascension model and give the steps logical sequential names like 'Silver', 'Gold' and 'Platinum'. Everyone knows what's more valuable.

Customer acquisition cost

Here's another marketing fundamental. The cost of acquiring a new customer is normally one of the highest costs in your business. It costs more to acquire a new customer than to sell to an existing customer. Once you understand and implement a strategic staircase, think how much more you could spend on marketing once you know the value of a customer. Your competition will be puzzled about how much you can spend on marketing, because they don't know your secret 'backend' - the higher steps of your staircase!

How To Create Your Own Product Staircase

Design Your Framework

First of all, as this concept is likely to be new to you, what do I mean by 'Framework' and why is it so important?

Definition of a Framework:

'A framework is a sequence of activities or steps you create that have helped your customers achieve results.'

In other words, a framework is a 'multi-part strategy that will lead your clients from point A to point B'. We live in the age where everyone is looking for a 'transformation' and your framework describes how your products or services help people achieve such a transformation: whether mentally, physically, monetarily or spiritually.

'Reverse-Engineer' your framework

You might not be aware of how you help your clients achieve these transformations, so if that is you - then it's time to 'reverse-engineer' your successes.

Simply list the steps you have taken and work out which steps your success stories have in common, and you will easily be able to create a framework of your own. This framework is your 'intellectual property' (IP) and will become a valuable asset in the future.

Especially if you grow your business and are thinking of licensing, franchising or are planning the sale of your business.

By putting your knowledge, expertise and know-how into a proprietary framework of activities you've devised, you will immediately position yourself as an Expert and have something unique to offer, which will make you more attractive to your prospective clients as a result.

Make it Unique and Memorable

A framework will help you with your own unique positioning in your industry. This is because your framework is based on your own personal philosophy, experience and success in achieving certain results, both for you and your clients.

Your framework should also have a unique and preferably memorable name. 'Expert Success' has it's own 3 Step Formula and it is *my* framework.

> *TopTip: Before you settle on a name, make sure its .com domain name is free and/or available. You'll only be disappointed when you find out later that it's gone.*

There are a number of words I recommend you can use to make your framework desirable. These include 'system', 'formula", 'method', 'blueprint', 'process' and 'methodology'. Any of these words will give your clients confidence that what you have to offer will lead them to the results they are looking for with certainty. Later in this chapter I will introduce you to the 'Framework Name Creator', which can help you in creating a powerful name for your framework.

Your Framework - the basis of all future Content and Product Creation

On of the most important reasons why you really need a framework is to clarify and prepare for your future product creation needs. This book, for example, and literally all of my courses and products are all derived from content and principles that are summed up in the 3 Step Formula to 'Expert Success'.

Similarly, your framework will help generate limitless ideas for all your future marketing campaigns, including articles, blog posts, videos, newsletters etc. As mentioned previously, your Expert positioning is not only based on your personal online brand, it's also defined through the quality of the products and services you offer that solve specific product problems for your clients.

Your personal and business philosophy

Your framework is one of the most powerful ways you can communicate your values. 'Expert Success' is a clear insight into my philosophy for success.

The concepts of 'expert positioning, creating powerful products and cultivating customers' are a clear demonstration of my values and philosophy.

Framework Case Study - Property Auction Insider Secrets

This product was initially launched with Property Auction Expert Ranjan Bhattacharya in 2010 as a six-week webinar course with two bonus weeks of additional content. The outcome of the course was to break down the process of how to buy successfully at property auctions. We broke this complex process down into "The Simple Six Step Process to Win at Property Auctions Guaranteed."

If you're familiar with property auctions then you'll know that buying at auction can be a minefield and there are hundreds of things to learn and remember. But by breaking the whole process down into our simple six step process made it conceptually very easy for anyone to follow, even a total novice! The program was a huge success and created over £100,000 in revenue.

Here are the six steps as broken down in this successful framework that generated multiple six figures for us in 2011:

Property Auction Framework: The "The Simple Six Step Process to Win at Property Auctions -Guaranteed."

Naming your Steps

Module 1: Pan for Gold.

(This means finding the right properties from the catalogue) As you can tell from the language used, it is universally recognised which people can relate to much better and that also has a strong emotional trigger. 'Panning For Gold' is something people can relate to and 'finding nuggets' – finding the few good bits within a plethora of possible answers.

I strongly believe that you must avoid using lingo specific to your niche at this stage, as you will alienate your prospects and will fail to connect with their needs.

Let me rush through the other steps quickly.

Module 2: Inspect & Survey.

Module 3: Navigate the Legal Maze.

Module 4: Determine Your Maximum Bid Price.

Module 5: Arrange Your Finance.

Module 6: Attending the Auction & Win.

Let me point out two commonalities of those steps and a guideline for creating your own framework.

1) Try to use action verbs whenever possible. 'Pan', 'inspect', 'navigating', 'determine', 'arrange' and 'attend' are all verbs that put people right at the centre of the action and help them to visualize the idea and believe they can do them as well.

2) Make sure the titles of each step are short sentences that have meaning by themselves.

Framework Case Study - The Expert Success Formula

'Expert Success Formula - A Simple 3-Step Formula to More Money, More Time and More Purpose'. It has three steps, which are short and memorable:

Step 1: Establish a Personal Online Brand

Step 2: Produce Powerful Products

Step 3: Cultivate a Buying Audience

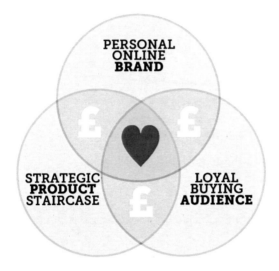

Again, you can clearly see that we use action verbs, 'establish', 'produce' and 'cultivate'. We've also used short sentences to simplify and therefore make it easier to understand.

Of course, like any other route to success or any successful product or service, there are hundreds of minor details in order to make these frameworks work, but its of utmost importance to give your prospects a very simple and memorable overview of what it is you'll be able to achieve for them.

Make it Memorable

It is very important that your framework is memorable. Here is the acid test: If your framework is so simple that your clients and customers can tell it to other people unaided, i.e. without your help, then you know you've got a decent framework.

Your best clients and customers will be your natural ambassadors who will spread the word about what you do, but you need to make it easy for them. Help them to tell your story to other people and a memorable, easy-to-explain framework is one of the key ways they can do that.

Using Alliteration

Alliteration can be a very powerful way to make your framework easier to remember, but it also can have its drawbacks. I have found that if your customer avatar is high net worth individuals, having the 'five Ps of successful investing' becomes more of an undesirable gimmick and might discredit your authority.

So depending on your situation, consider alliteration, but be aware of the possible downfalls.

'Naming' Your Framework

1	2	3	4	5	6	7	8	9
				process				
	little known			system				
	secret	3		formula				
	proven	4	step	blueprint		(your benefit)		(timeframe)
The	tried and tested	5	part	pillars	to	e.g. mastering	in	e.g. 30 days
	simple	6	-	cornerstones		pottery		
	easy	7		ingredients				
	...			path				
				methodology				

The 'Framework Name Creator' helps you get started. Just use one word from each column to have a great sounding Framework: e.g. 'The Little Known 5 Step Process To Mastering The Art of Pottery In 30 Days'.

Using Visual Aids

Visual aids are also very powerful tools. In his famous book 'Rich Dad, Poor Dad', Robert Kiyosaki created a framework from an easy-to-remember, polarized view of the world. His powerful visual aid is called the 'Cash Flow Quadrant', and I am sure if you've read the book, you'll remember the 'Quadrant'.

This visual aid helps the reader to understand his framework and, breaks the information down into simple steps by dividing the world into four quadrants.

It put Robert on the map, made him a recognized expert and he has used the same 'framework' in literally all of his books, courses and programs.

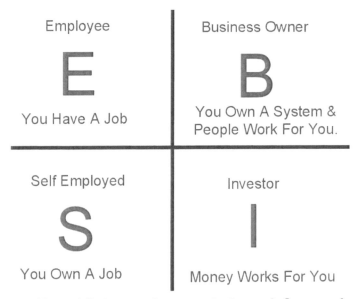

Robert Kiyosaki's famous framework, the cash flow quadrant, which became the basis of literally all his products and teachings including his many books.

EXERCISE:
Create Your Own Framework

Now that you're clear what a framework is and why it's so important, use the 3 simple steps to create your own compelling framework.

1. Reverse Engineer Your Results

The first one is to reverse engineer the results that you have achieved for your clients and work backwards to identify how you helped them get those results.

You might be a weight-loss coach, you might be an executive trainer, you might be planting potatoes, but whatever it is that you achieve there are certain steps, often called 'unconscious competencies' that you use to achieve those results.

Write down the results you are able or will be to achieve for you clients or future clients. Remember people are looking for transformation in their lives, the A -> B.

_____

_____

_____

_____

_____

_____

_____

2. Break It Down into Steps

Now that you have your results, break down your process of achieving those results into steps. This will help you and your client to simplify what it is that they need to do.

My advice would be to break it down into less than seven primary steps. I would try to stick with three, four or five. (But we're talking about 'primary steps' only, of course. There are many possible 'sub-steps' that you can share with your prospects later on as they consume your products and services).

1 _____

_____

2 _____

_____

3 _____

_____

4 _____

_____

5 _____

_____

6 _____

_____

7 _____

_____

3. Give It A Name

Using the Framework Name Creator, simply complete the following 3 steps.

1. choose one value per column

2. add your benefit (column 7)

3. add your timeframe (optional) (column 9)

1	2	3	4	5	6	7	8	9
The	little known secret proven tried and tested simple easy ...	3 4 5 6 7	step part -	process system formula blueprint pillars cornerstones ingredients path methodology	to	(your benefit) e.g. mastering pottery	in	(timeframe) e.g. 30 days

_____

_____

_____

_____

_____

_____

_____

Define The Steps

Once your framework outline is complete, it's time to define the steps of your staircase. This is important because you want to create the best possible match for the different needs of your different client profiles. This allows you to offer the right product, to the right person and at the right time – and in doing so, maximizing your lifetime customer value.

Staircase Examples

Let me show you a real life example from my own coaching business, where I have tweaked and implemented a 'product staircase'. I offer different levels of coaching/membership to allow easy entry to our group, but also enough opportunities to upgrade and ascend to meet almost every level of coaching need for our clients.

Logically, the higher levels of coaching demand a higher financial investment from our clients and a higher time investment from myself and our Expert Success Certified Coaches.

The staircase starts with the 'Silver Level' and moves all the way to 'Diamond'. Access to the 'Mastermind Program' at the top of the staircase is on application only. The only services outside this staircase are bespoke consulting and private coaching.

The reason we describe our services as a 'staircase' and not the traditional word 'marketing funnel' is because different clients will start their journey at different places.

The Expert Success Academy

Level	Silver	Gold	Platinum	Diamond	Mastermind
Monthly Newsletter	✔	✔	✔	✔	✔
Monthly Audio CD	✔	✔	✔	✔	✔
Monthly Coaching Webinar	✘	✔	✔	✔	✔
Access to Membership Site & Archive	✘	✔	✔	✔	✔
Private Face Book Group	✘	✔	✔	✔	✔
Monthly Live Meeting London	✘	✘	✔	✔	✔
Minimum 30% Discount on all Courses	✘	✘	✔	✔	✔
Monthly Live Group Coaching	✘	✘	✘	✔	✔
Weekly Group Coaching Calls	✘	✘	✘	✔	✔
Monthly Mastermind Meeting	✘	✘	✘	✘	✔
Monthly 1:1 Calls	✘	✘	✘	✘	✔
2 Day Retreat	✘	✘	✘	✘	✔
Direct 999 Access	✘	✘	✘	✘	✔

The 'Product Staircase' of our Expert Success Academy Coaching program. Mapping out progression and levels is key. You might have to play around and tweak them over time, but levels have been proven to increase results for our customers and our bottom line.

Our 'Mastermind' is - as mentioned - an application only program. But it doesn't matter if you have previously been a 'Silver', 'Gold', 'Platinum' or 'Diamond' member. Having said that, we have found that most of our current 'Mastermind Members' have been natural graduates of Platinum and Diamond. This again demonstrates the power of ascension, as many people join the lower levels and then upgrade to 'Platinum' or 'Diamond'.

We'll talk more later about repurposing existing content, but a multi-level coaching program is a great example where some of the content we create in one level is re-used and re-purposed for other levels. Re-purposing content leverages your time, your resources and increases your lifetime customer value.

How To Design Your Own Product Staircase

I am sure you're now itching to define your own steps of your product staircase now that you have your framework. Before I let you do the exercise, let me give you some more clues and tips how to get this done. I have broken this down into 4 steps:

- Map Existing Products

- Identify Any Gaps

- Fill In Gaps For Logical Progression

- Create A New 'Super Level' Product Or Service

1 – Map your Existing Products

If you have existing products or services, simply map them into a matrix. Any spreadsheet or mindmap will do. I prefer spreadsheets for this type of matrix, because I can easily add columns and rows to suit.

Write down what type of products they are, what type of access to you and your staff those products need, and which pricing category they belong to. Here are some categories to help you map your existing products.

- What is it you have that is free?

- What could serve as a TRUST transaction?

- What could serve as a MID TICKET transaction?

- What could serve as a HIGH TICKET transaction?

- How much of your time do these products require?

None for: No Access to you needed,
Mixed for: Some Access to you needed,
Full Access for: You have to be there!

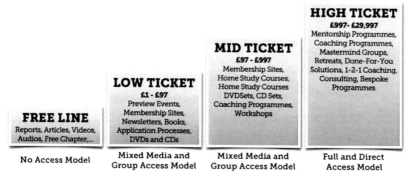

Most Product Staircases in the service professionals industry
have a similar structure.

2 - Identify any Gaps

Some of your clients will go through their journey from your free offer all the way up to your highest-level product. Much of your staircase will be refined and tweaked once you can test and measure it with real data (people!).

Let me tell you a story of my good friend Rob Moore, who has been a strategic business partner of mine for the last five years. When he came to my Product Creation Workshop in 2007, Rob Moore and his company Progressive Property had two products at two extreme ends of a product staircase.

First they had a successful book about property investing retailing around £15, then they had a £60,000 passive investment hands-free portfolio-buying product, with nothing in between.

By identifying gaps within that product staircase, Rob Moore and his company were able to multiply the profit and turnover of the company. If you look at that business model today, you'll see that they have filled the gaps with a range of products, courses and services. Many of them low or mid range in price and most of them with no or mixed access to Rob and his core team.

3 – Fill the Gaps for a Logical Progression

If you have mapped out your existing products and services, you'll have probably found some gaps. Spot those gaps and create logical products and services that will fill them. Ask yourself these questions:

- What do your different clients need to get started? (Depending on demographic, budget and geography, etc)

- What is their logical progression? (Where would they start and where do you want to them to end up)

- What do they need to progress to the next level? (what level of success on their behalf, what kind of marketing will you need to have in place, etc.)

4 – Create a new 'Super Level' product or service

This is a really hot tip for everyone, whether you're a beginner or an experienced product creator. No matter what you offer currently, I urge you to create a new, higher-value, premium-priced product.

Firstly, there's always a part of your database and your clients that want more of you, your products and your knowledge. This aspirational part of your client database is ready to step up to the next level, right away. They'll also be prepared to pay premium prices for more access.

Secondly, it's essential for all the rest of your clients (the majority) to know that there's always more. You as the leader and they as the tribe are always on a journey to bigger and better things!

The third welcome side effect to having this high price 'super-product' is that it creates a contrast frame. All your existing products will suddenly appear much better value in comparison to the newly created 'super-level'. Creating a contrast frame is one of the key ways to influence a person's behavior, so don't underestimate the power of this strategy.

Finally, it really helps you to stretch your own comfort zone. Allowing yourself to charge more for your expertise, products or services is more a psychological comfort zone breaker than anything else.

1,000% pay rise anyone?

When I started my one day workshops back in 2006, I charged £147 for a full day hands on workshop. After much pushing from my coaches and peers, I was able to raise my prices (without much change to the content) to £297, £497, £697 and £897 without a decline in uptake within 18 months. I then extended it to a two day workshop with the same material and charged up to £1,497 within another 12 months. In essence I was able to raise my prices by 1,000% within two and a half years. Ironically I had more success and better students when I charged more for my products and services!

Creating Higher Levels

In January 2013 I took my 10 Inner Circle Mastermind students to a weekend retreat in Portugal. While my UK tribe was looking on, we had a few glorious days in the sun (just another reason to run those types of groups).

What is fascinating though is that the Inner Circle Mastermind is the highest level of my Coaching Program the Expert Success Academy. (It's £15,000 for a year).

I always offer the opportunity to renew their membership at these retreats but was aware that there was 'nowhere to go' from Mastermind. I had a quick think and created a 'Mastermind PLUS' and a 'Mastermind EXTREME' level (being mainly a decoy level).

The results speak for themselves. 60% took me up on the PLUS level, which didn't even exist a week before!

How to create a Super Level

If you're wondering how to create these super levels, here are a couple of suggestions:

1. Try bundling together several of your existing products. Create a special package and sell that at a higher price point.

2. If you offer services or experiential events, create luxury retreats in an exotic location. This is a very high growth area in many different industries, as people are increasingly willing to pay premium prices for experiences that combine holidays and leisure with a health or other related interest.

   My good friend Jamie Smart, has created many high priced retreats for the transformational market of coaching. Whether it's life or business, there's a lot to be gained from intense bursts of activity over a short period of time. Another benefit Jamie tells me is that he loves holidaying in exotic locations so why not enjoy what you love doing, create tremendous value for your clients and get paid all at the same time.

3. Charge upfront for a product or service over a period of time. For example you may charge for twelve months access to a

membership site or twelve months access to a networking group, but by allowing people to pay up front for their year you can charge a higher price.

Our 'Mastermind' level is a good example of this strategy. It is a high-ticket monthly coaching program over a fixed-term period paid up front. So, instead of charging £1,000 per month for private coaching, we made it an application only product with two intakes a year and a limit for 12 businesses only and we charge £6,000 +vat for the six-month program upfront.

4. Combine your teachings with a 'Done-For-You' solution. This always adds value which is easy to demonstrate. The Executive Brand Makeover program is such an example. At £12,000 - £18,000 it includes many parts that are done for the client.

5. Add a ' Business Opportunity Element' to your offer. Our Expert Success Coach Certification is in essence a high ticket course that includes a 'business opportunity'. Being able to teach and use my framework and materials allows any Expert Success Coach to make potentially tens of thousands of pounds a year in extra income.

EXERCISE:
Create A Product Staircase

Use a spreadsheet or a large piece of paper:

1. Map Existing Products

Write down all your existing products and services that you currently offer/sell. If you are just starting out, just make things up and have at least five products and/or services which are related or sequential and fit into the low, mid and high price categories.

2. Identify Any Gaps

Identify the gaps you need to fill. Simply split it into low, mid and high price products and work out access levels needed to you and your team. Assign no, mixed and full access levels to your products

3. Fill Gaps for Logical Progression

Brainstorm logical products and services you could offer to your clients that would fill those gaps, taking into account different customer profiles and criteria mentioned earlier.

4. Create a new 'Super Level' product or service

'Dream up' a new high-end premium priced product or service you could offer. Don't worry about who's going to buy it or how affordable it is or how you're going to sell it.

Create it, make it real and available and see what happens.

Plan Your Revenue

Now that you've designed your framework and mapped out the steps in our product staircase, it's time for a sanity check. You need to plan the revenue that these product staircase steps are going to generate for your business.

This is an important step to check that what you've designed and created fits in with the aspirations and goals you've set for your lifestyle, your business model and your ideal clients.

I've seen many people throw random numbers around for revenue targets. They've never actually sat down and worked out to see if the products and services they have available can actually create their revenue goals.

Here are a couple of tips and tricks for you to calculate your revenue plan:

Revenue by time period

Breakdown the revenue you want to achieve, (for example, £120,000) over a time period of 12 months. It makes sense to plan in years or tax years, as these are units that your business will be charged tax for. Its also good practice to work with annual plans, as well as to break those down further into four quarters, (i.e. 90-day chunks).

Revenue by product

Now that you've broken your revenue target down into time periods, you should also breakdown your revenue targets or expectations by product. How many sales of each individual product in your staircase will you need to make in order to achieve your desired results? Now play around with the numbers to find the optimum balance between product price value and transaction frequency until you think you can achieve those revenue targets. Be realistic about conversion numbers from one step of your staircase to another.

Revenue by fulfillment time

Look at the breakdown of products and services and mark how long it would take you to fulfill a single one of them, including excellent customer service and follow ups. Then work out how much time it will take you and your team to fulfill the number you specified. Do this for all the products and services.

Just a clue. You don't have 24 hours a day and 365 days a year. I would work on a maximum of 5 hours a day and 200 days a year, meaning 1000 billable hours. The rest will be taken up by running and managing the business and your well deserved breaks.

Revenue by amount of prospects

A second question would be how many prospects will you need to make those sales? You'll not be able to predict exactly how many people will migrate from one level to another, but you can look at industry averages as well as your existing statistics to calculate how many prospects you need to make a sale.

My tip is to be conservative in your estimates and surprise yourself with better results as you progress. Be careful not to be over-ambitious or set yourself up for failure or disappointment. Set high targets while still being realistic.

Estimate the cost of acquisition, of customers and fulfillment

Last but not least, it makes sense to factor in the cost of acquiring a customer and fulfillment for those products and services you need to sell. This includes things such as venue hire, materials, staff, affiliates, sales people and marketing costs.

I've seen businesses go broke because they've sold products without taking into consideration the cost of fulfilling the product or service. Many have gone bankrupt while trying to fulfill those promises over a period of time, especially if the money was collected upfront.

NOTE:
For your convenience I have put all the exercises into an easy to download and easy to print pdf file. It's better than writing in the book :-) just go to following url to download it: http://ExpertSuccessBook.com/workbook

EXERCISE:
Plan Your Revenue

Create a simple spreadsheet. Create columns for the months and rows for your products.

Once you have done that, break down your desired revenue in the following sections:

Breakdown Your Revenue by Time Period

Breakdown Your Revenue by Product

Breakdown Your Revenue by Fulfillment Time

Breakdown Your Revenue by Amount of Prospects Needed

Estimate the Cost of Acquisition of Customers and Fulfillment

PS: You can download my simple Revenue Calculator.

Go to http://ExpertSuccessBook.com/calculator

	FREE	LOW TICKET	MID TICKET	HIGH TICKET	Monthly	Per year
Price	£0	£20	£297	£1,497		
People	500	50	10	2		
Conversion		10%	20%	20%		
Revenue		£1,000	£2,970	£2,994	£6,964	£83,568
Cost		£500	£1,000	£1,000	£2,500	£30,000
Profit		£500	£1,970	£1,994	**£4,464**	**£53,568**

2.2 Create Powerful Products

Now that you've mapped your product staircase it's time to look at the different options you have available to create some high value products fast. In this section we'll look at different product creation models, utilize multiple media to maximize reach and success rate of your products and we'll explore some smart re-purposing strategies that will cut your product creation time drastically.

Product Creation Models

1. The Author Model

This is where you create the content yourself. Most people think this is the only way. Creating your own product has some unique benefits.

An example is the book you're reading now: 'Expert Success' has been 100% written and created by me, 'the author'.

Can Be Fast And You're 100% In Control

One of the perceptions about 'making your own products' is that they take more time to create. But creating your own products can be quick and easy – because you're in full control of the content, copyright, publishing and distribution. One downside to this and possibly the greatest single danger with this model is that most people never, ever complete their products! That is why I always publish to a date or deadline.

One key reason I have found is that people expect it to be perfect straight away. And that expectation actually stops them from ever completing their product. I can relate! In the process of publishing this book I have had my own expectation of 'creating the perfect book'.

Another possible reason to delay or procrastinate the completion of your product is the lack of belief in your own ability to produce a product that is 'good enough'. You know more than you think and this unconscious competence can stop you in your tracks!

The most important thing about products is that they are available! They have to be out there. Unless they're out there for sale you can't make any money from them

If you know a decent amount about your subject matter you'll be able to produce something of similar or superior quality to much of the material out there. If you recall the Expert Success Matrix and you are positioned anywhere above the bottom 25%, you'll be just fine! Also consider that the content is only part of the equation. It's in the marketing and the context you create where your true success lies.

The Expert Success Matrix™

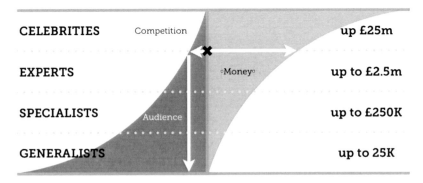

CELEBRITIES	Competition	up £25m
EXPERTS	°Money°	up to £2.5m
SPECIALISTS	Audience	up to £250K
GENERALISTS		up to 25K

The money is distributed based on your position on the matrix, not based on the knowledge you have! Perception is Reality!

Here is a little trick to deal with the twin evils of procrastination and perfectionism: Set yourself a 'hard' deadline to get your project published by, whatever may happen.

To stick to your deadline, one method I always use is to find accountability partners. They are not necessarily collaborators but could be a coach or friend that help you stay on track, just like your personal trainer in the gym.

Another way that helps me meet my deadlines is to announce my plans and product releases publicly. To your tribe, on video, your friends. It doesn't really matter who you announce it to - but what does matter is that you make it public.

2. The Collaboration Model

The second common model of producing products is a collaboration model, where you work together with someone. I have plenty of examples in my portfolio. Interview products like 'Property Habits' that I released in 2005 with Parmdeep Vadesha contained audio interviews with 12 Property Experts. This product was co-produced and is co-owned. Proceeds of the sale are split.

One obvious advantage is having your accountability partner as part of your product creation team. If you choose to co-own and co-create, just make sure you have your agreement in writing. This doesn't have to be a big legal document, but just make sure you have a clear understanding of who does what, split of cost and fulfillment and of course, profits.

Easy To Get Started

What I particularly like about this model is that it is generally a fast and easy way to get started if you're completely new to creating information products. In fact, this is the method that we've been teaching our students in the Expert Success Academy with great success.

Interview products are generally an easy way to get expert opinions and knowledge into an easy-to-consume and easy-to-publish model. Transcriptions from those interviews are quick to produce and allow you to split the content into articles, and reports and other useful marketing material.

3. The Publisher Model

The Publisher model is where someone creates all the content for you and you act as the publisher with full rights to the content and to sell the product. In my early days I commissioned a dog training eBook that was written by a ghostwriter and published under a pen name. So I paid someone to actually create the product, then once completed, they agreed to assign exclusive copyright to me for its sale.

This might sound like a difficult way for people when they get started. Many find it especially difficult not to be personally involved with the content of their product. In my case it wasn't really by choice, as I really knew nothing about dog training.

My first ever e-book, 'Who's The Top Dog' was ghost written and published under a pen name. It made me over $23,000 and built me a list of hundreds of buyers within just weeks.

To have people create content doesn't mean you have to publish them faceless or under a pen name.

If you're able to take advantage of this model and you have the money to invest in the creation of the product, it is a fast way to get your products up and running, and with a great leverage of your time.

One way to use this strategy is to have other people research topics or bring together information that you finally put together. That way you leverage your time and at the same time control the content and can put your name to it.

Utilising Multiple Media For Your Products

Another important factor in product creation is how to best utilize multiple media to create products that complete your 'Product Staircase'.

What do i mean by 'Multiple Media'?

'Multiple Media refers to the practice of using more than one (multiple) channel of communication (media) to contact customers and prospects.'

Learning style considerations

The use of multiple media is important for a number of reasons.

People prefer different learning styles.

1. Some people prefer to learn visually and therefore like reading books or watching videos.

2. Some people are more auditory learners and prefer listening to audio CDs or MP3 downloads.

3. Others - kinesthetic learners - prefer the physical experience such as going to seminars and workshops in person.

Now we are all a bit of everything but we all have a preferred way of consuming information. By appealing to all learning styles you naturally stand a better chance of engaging more of your prospects and customers.

In fact, science has identified seven different learning styles which I have listed below. You can easily see how different media will appeal to those styles.

1. **Visual** (spatial): You prefer using pictures, images, and spatial understanding.

2. **Aural** (auditory-musical): You prefer using sound and music.

3. **Verbal** (linguistic): You prefer using words, both in speech and writing.

4. **Physical** (kinesthetic): You prefer using your body, hands and sense of touch.

5. **Logical** (mathematical): You prefer using logic, reasoning and systems.

6. **Social** (interpersonal): You prefer to learn in groups or with other people.

7. **Solitary** (intrapersonal): You prefer to work alone and use self-study.

Modalities considerations

The use of multiple media allows you to share the same information in different 'modalities' of learning, thereby repeating and reinforcing your message multiple times. It often requires multiple instances of people consuming your content before they a) understand it fully and b) follow it to get the best results for themselves.

Efficiency considerations

The use of multiple media allows you to re-use and re-purpose your content. Which means you don't have to create as many products as you might think! For example, if you've created some video content you can repurpose it by stripping out the audio and transcribing the content.

Media type considerations

At this stage we're talking about how to market any information product, from a simple lead generation device through to a high-end physical product or service. Information products provide a very profitable income stream for any Expert business.

Printed Media

Physically printed products include books such as 'Expert Success' are essential to your Product Staircase. Print media can include reports or white papers which you may offer for free or low price to acquire a customer. It also includes newsletters like the 'Expert Success' newsletter, which is a monthly publication available to all members of the 'Expert Success Academy'.

Auditory Media

Auditory media includes physical CDs, such as the monthly 'Expert Success CD' that I publish alongside the 'Expert Success' newsletter. It can also refer to the digital equivalents of the CD, such as MP3 downloads, live-streaming via the web or podcasts. Members can access many different audio recordings in our private membership site.

Podcasts are another way to deliver audio products. Podcasts allow you to publish and your clients to subscribe to a series of digital recordings available via download to your mp3 player or computer. Podcasts can be free or paid for, but most people I know use it as a free lead generator, bonus or upsell.

Auditory media also includes Teleseminars, which were extremely popular when I got started in 2005, but have since slowly been pushed into the background by Webinars.

Visual Media

Recent innovations in technology and internet connection speeds have made streaming video an obvious choice for providing content.

Although online video is dominating the way people consume content, we also create and sell physical DVD products. Such as the recordings of our yearly Industry event the 'Expert Success Summit'.

One of the most powerful uses of online video however is webinars, both live and automated. Webinars consist normally of either a PowerPoint slideshow or a recording of a computer screen. This is a fantastic medium to deliver training, coaching or indeed sales presentations of any sort. I have found that a mindmap is a quick and compelling way to share information on a webinar, foregoing the need to spend ages doing powerpoint slides.

Webinars can be free, paid-for individually, or delivered as part of a mid-range coaching program. They also make great bonuses, either for your own products or when promoting someone else's in a joint venture. They provide great leverage at little to no fulfillment cost and have no geographic constraints.

I've used webinars successfully to sell anything from $1 trials through to £15,000 per year coaching programs, and they can be used in most businesses to great effect.

Another great advantage – especially when you are starting out – is that people don't know if there are hundred or ten people on your webinar. If you ran a physical event, it'd be blindingly obvious if you only had ten people there and you'd have the risk of high costs for the hotel or workshop.

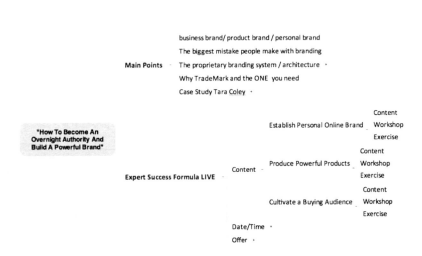

You can open and close branches of the mindmap on a webinar to reveal and hide information and content. And they are quicker to create than Powerpoint.

Experiential Media

It is particularly relevant for the kinesthetic learner that you provide and deliver content through Experiential Media. Kinesthetic learners need to have a physical 'immersion' in the subject matter in order to fully learn information.

Some examples of experiential media include small workshops, large seminars, one-to-one or group coaching, and high-end luxury retreats.

I just love physical events. Here is me on stage in London. Apart from speaking to 700+ people and selling £50,000 of my products and services I also sold over 100 books and connected personally with hundreds of people. I can't even put a monetary value on this. Many of the people in the room will eventually become customers of mine.

Although there are greater costs and risks involved in running those physical events, I have found that the 'stick rate' – the length of time your customers stay in your community or program, is greatly increased with physical events.

Why I love Experiential Media

Firstly, I can testify that I experienced literally all of my personal and business breakthroughs in live events.

Secondly, it takes more commitment from both parties, meaning you'll have more committed people in the room.

Thirdly, you have more control over the environment your clients are in when they consume your content.

Content Repurposing Strategies

Having multiple products is one of the most important parts of your 'Expert Success'. Your authority in your industry will largely derive from the products that you make available.

Therefore, being able to produce multiple quality products, quickly and inexpensively, will increase your authority and sales and give you the flexibility to create many different bundle and bonus combinations.

Let's look at other ways of repurposing your products and content in more detail.

Repurposing Your Own Content

A classic strategy is to run a live event and have it filmed. First you hold the event, which as we've discussed is an experiential product. Then you have the event recorded on video in order to create a number of new products derived from the same core material.

The '3-In-One' Live Event Content Repurpose Strategy

As soon as your event has been filmed, you can create a video-based product from it such as a DVD box set or set up online access to the digital video version.

Next, you strip out the audio from the DVD set to create an audio product, such as a set of physical CDs, or downloadable MP3s.

Finally, you can transcribe those audios to produce written reports, articles or blog posts.

All three products now have the same or similar content, but can be sold at different price points to different segments of your market on different occasions. By doing this, you allow people to choose the format they prefer to consume your information.

> *TopTip: Create special additional bonuses to each product (DVD, Audio, Transcript). This means that people will buy multiple products although they contain a lot of the same content in different media.*

The '3-In-One' Webinar Content Repurpose Strategy

You can also repurpose content from a webinar series. This is possible whether you're the author of the content, or if you're just hosting the webinar in conjunction with guest experts. You can use the knowledge of other experts to create a value-packed live webinar series, that is a product in its own right.

However, you also apply the '3-in-one' content repurposing strategy to webinars as well as live events. Once the webinar series has been delivered, you can take those recordings and turn them into a video DVD product, an audio CD product as well as a digital online membership site available by streaming or download.

I've used this model many times. I helped run a jointly owned product called 'Property Auction Insider Secrets', which was a six-week live webinar series. The webinars were recorded and turned into a physical DVD video box set and an accompanying online membership site allowing for interaction with the customers. The mix of products was able to generate over £100,000 in mostly automated sales for us. If we had only run the webinar series, it would have been less than £50,000 (still great but why leave money on the table?)

Live events and live webinar models are just two ways you can create content in one media, and repurpose the same information into other media to create new products and increase sales.

Other People's Content

A fast and cheap way to create products is to use other people's existing content via a licensing deal. Licensing effectively means that you purchase the rights to legally use someone else's product, content and the right to sell it.

Three Most Common Licensing Deals

There are many different types of licensing agreements. Here are three common ones:

Resale Rights

This is where you purchase the rights to take someone else's product and sell it as if it were your own. Often resale rights products come with sales material such as a sales letter and even an email follow-up sequence that you can customize very quickly. In this way you can have a product for sale almost immediately.

Master Resale Rights

This is less common, but this type of license allows you to sell on the resale rights of the product to someone else. Effectively, you become the person selling resale rights of a particular product to other people.

Private Label Rights

It allows you to take other people's content and do almost anything with it you like. You might like to repackage it, repurpose it, edit it and sell it as your own. You can customize the product with your own name or brand, thereby creating a completely unique product as a result.

2 Ways to use Private Label Rights content to create your own products

Here are two ways that you can use 'Private Label Rights' content to create your own products:

1. Take an existing product and rebrand it only. Change the author's name from the original author to yourself. You might want to change the title of the product as well but nothing else. Congratulations, you now have your own product to sell! This is by far the fastest way to create a product that is 100% unique to you. Be sure that it is good content if you put your name to it!

2. Convert the product to a different media. This second strategy is one used by only a handful of marketers, as it leverages the 'multiple media' product creation strategy we discussed earlier.

I recently bought some great slides on marketing mistakes and made it into a video series. I changed some of the content, all of the branding and recorded them as videos. It cost me $17 to buy the slides and I was able to create hours of good value beginners' content.

Using licensed materials or private label rights is a great idea as a starting point. Many times it will help you to get over the initial fear of product creation we all initially have. Once you have some content to work with, it's relatively easy to customize it by adding your own twist, knowledge and experience in order to make the product distinctly your own.

2.3 Increase Product Value

I mentioned earlier that the content of the products is of course important and I trust you have a range of products that work and create a difference in peoples' lives. But it's not only the content of your material that will determine the success of your products, it's also how you package and present them.

Packaging increases the perceived value of the product to your targeted customer. In this section I'll be talking about how you can increase that perceived value. I'm also going to show you how to create highly compelling offers.

In my mind creating a compelling offer is a way of 'packaging the product'. The offer is displaying the benefits and value of the product.

We are all susceptible to 'packaging'. The packaging and the image that manufacturers are able to create in the customer's mind have become far more important than the actual content. When selling products online or selling physical products, we need to play by the same rules.

Coffee is another great example. People buy into the brand, be it Starbucks, Costa or Nero, and are willing to pay multiple times the 'value' because of its brand and packaging.

Starbucks or Polystyrene Cup? In Starbucks case costing you around £3 compared to the 50p brew at Joe's breakfast place. In Starbucks case the value of the actual content (the coffee) equates to just 3% of its total price.

We can see from premium brands in the market that packaging is always far more important compared to lower quality brands.

Creating Higher Perceived Value

Graphics

Let's look at graphics first. Graphics do matter. It's highly important to make sure everything you share with the outside world supports the brand values you stand for. This is especially so when you sell products online, because sometimes a product graphic is the only thing people can see before they are asked to make a buying decision.

For every digital product I sell, I always have a physical box set graphic created. Every eBook or report has a physical book cover and every downloadable audio has a CD or DVD box cover to enhance the perceived value of the product.

Watch your own buying habits

So when you browse for an information product or services next time, ask yourself 'why did I buy?' and 'what made me feel comfortable with that decision?' Almost invariably you'll find that either a high quality product design or some element of branding has created the trust and the desire to buy that product over a competitor. You need to do the same too.

The 7-Figure Formula DVD Set Graphics. It's important you create high value graphics for your products.

A common challenge when trying to convey the value of an online product is that they have no 'thud' value. This term describes the sound a product makes when you slam it onto the desk or kitchen table. eBooks, digital audios and downloadable videos have no 'thud' value. So you must create an image in your customer's mind of the 'thud' value of the products that you offer. This will increase the perceived value of the product and make you more money.

Bundling & splitting products

A great way to increase perceived value is to bundle products together. Here is where the product creation strategy of re-purposing comes in very handy. You can sell a video product and add the audio version and the transcripts as a bundle to create a better, or easier to consume product at literally no extra cost to you.

Another easy strategy for increasing perceived value is splitting products. For example, let's imagine you have one core product on a particular topic that you were intending to sell as a complete product, such as an eBook.

What you might want to do instead is to remove a number of chapters of that eBook from the core product and use them as special bonuses or special supplementary reports. This effectively makes them additional products in their own right. What you've done is to add increased value to your proposition. The package now consists of the core eBook plus these additional bonus reports, which all contribute to a higher perceived value.

Instead of creating overwhelm it's better to focus on the core benefit and create a product about a single core benefit, and then offer the other benefits as 'free' bonuses to increase perceived value and help them make a purchase decision.

Switching to media of higher perceived value

Another simple strategy to increase the perceived value of your product is to use more valuable media. To illustrate this, let me ask you a question. Which information is more valuable? The information in an eBook or the information in a physical book? Information delivered via webinar or the information at a live event? Information in a downloadable video or on the DVD sent to your home?

We all have a feeling that certain media has higher inherent value, in this case the book, the physical DVD sent to your home or the live event. Yet the delivery of the content via its media is totally separate from the actual information you wish to share.

So if you have a choice of media, choose the media that has the highest possible perceived value to deliver your content. This allows you to charge significantly higher prices.

> *TopTip: If your product includes multiple media, multiple events and multiple experiences, then you can't easily be compared like for like. This can give you a unique positioning advantage in any market.*

How To Create A Compelling Offer

You need to create a compelling offer because the vast majority of the success of your sales will be based on the strength of that offer, not the product in itself. This is why this is another important section for you to pay attention to.

In effect the combination of conditions of the sale constitutes the offer. That's what makes it compelling to buy that particular car at that particular time. You can do the same with your product.

Five characteristics of a compelling offer

1) High Perceived Value

Let's start with the most important characteristic of all, high perceived value. Now naturally the perception of high value is judged by your prospect and not you or anyone else.

One of the easiest ways to express the value of your product or service is to use the following phrase 'if you give me X, I'll give you Y.' For example, 'if you give me £195+vat I'll give you lifetime access to my most popular online-video home-study program that will show you step-by-step how to build an online business from scratch in 30 days or less'.

If you articulate your value proposition in a similar way and do not feel as if your customer is getting an absolute bargain then you need to either review your offer, or at least review the way you present its perceived value.

High perceived value is important irrespective of price point. I pay as much attention to the perceived value of our £47 Expert Success Academy Gold Program as to our £15,000 Mastermind level.

2) Credibility

The second characteristic of irresistible offers is credibility. This is because before people will buy 'from' you, they need to buy 'into' you. One of the easiest and fastest shortcuts to create your own personal credibility is to create a high-quality personal online brand, and position yourself as an Expert.

3) Believability

The third characteristic of irresistible offers is believability. In this case its not so much about you personally, but rather how readily your prospects believe that your offer is realistic and believable.

This is also why you have to give explicit reasons for discounts and why a product is available at all. You might have detected your own mind thinking: 'If it's all so great, why are you giving it away?'

4) Completeness

The fourth characteristic of irresistible offers is completeness. This means you need to give your prospects all the information they need that is RELEVANT to allow them to make a buying decision.

This is the reason why its necessary sometimes to create long-form sales letters, run 60 minute webinars or make 90 minute live presentations, because the offer has to be complete and might include some necessary education to allow your prospects to understand the value.

5) Clarity

The fifth and final key characteristic of your irresistible offer is clarity. You can provide the greatest case ever-made for your 'meritorious offer', but if you're not clearly stating what you want your prospect to do next then all the effort will been in vain.

In short, you need to spell-out the exact steps the prospect needs to take in order to take advantage of your compelling offer. It may be to complete an application or order form. It may be to click on the 'Big Orange Button' and enter your payment details on the following page. It may be to call your office number between two specific times and ask to speak to a specific member of your team.

It may seem obvious, but again, you'd be amazed how many people forget this vital element.

Let's look at even more ways to making your offer more compelling: We'll explore the use of bonuses and scarcity, the use of a contrast frame and different plausible reasons for your special offer.

The use of Bonuses

A simple strategy you can use is to create additional products purely to give away as bonuses, another is to split out your core product to offer the product plus a number of bonuses. Here are some more ways to use bonuses.

Free Lifetime Updates

If you're offering information products, particularly if it is an online product, you can offer 'free lifetime updates'. Let's say you were publishing an eBook. If you were to occasionally update that eBook, you could offer people the ability to download the updated version for free. There is real perceived value in that opportunity.

If you're offering a membership site where people can access content on a particular topic, you can give them free lifetime access. Lifetime is a long time and has high perceived value. People are reassured by the fact that they can get access to that product forever after the point of purchase. Of course it doesn't have to be 'forever' and you'd be wise to have Ts&Cs outlining that the free updates refer to the lifetime of the product, not the lifetime of the customer!

One of the great advantages of bonuses like that is that there's no extra cost for you. You keep developing your product anyway and delivering updates on eBooks or software for member access is actually part of your normal product development. Plus, the delivery of those to your existing customers is often free or a very low cost. The moment of delivery of your product is the perfect moment to offer an upsell, an additional product or ask them for a favor to help you with a survey to find out more about your customer's interests.

Fast Start Guides

Another great idea for a high perceived value bonus is a 'fast start guide'. This is a great bonus because people love to feel as if they can get started fast in consuming the content for whatever they buy.

A fast start guide can simply be a two page report and that details what people need to do to get started quickly. This is very inexpensive and easy to create. It's also very self serving because a fast start guide will make sure people will actually start using your product or service, get results quicker and therefore will be buying other products and will talk about the experience they had with your product. It also helps to reduce refund rates and increase future purchases.

The use of Scarcity

Another highly compelling part of every offer I've ever created or that I helped create for our clients is a concept called 'scarcity'. If you haven't read Dr Robert Cialdini's book called 'Influence' yet, please do so! If you have read it, let me remind you that scarcity is a genetically programmed driver of human action based on our fear of 'missing out'.

Scarcity has been used in a wide variety of sales and marketing processes for many hundreds of years. There are a couple of useful distinctions around scarcity that I'd like to share, starting with the different types of scarcity you can use.

Time Based Scarcity

Time based scarcity is a classic tactic used the world over to help sell products of all kinds. Just look at Disney for example, who release their DVDs for a limited period of time and then take them off the market again. Similarly, they also only release 'special editions' of certain classic films for a short time. This means that when it's available, people will take action because they don't want to miss out. Once they're gone, they're gone.

An easy and believable way of using scarcity is to link your offer to a particular holiday or event date. If you have an offer for a particular product, which is available up until a natural event like Christmas, Easter or Halloween, then people immediately know and understand when those dates are, and so they tend to remember them more easily.

This is why I always advise my clients to run their marketing calendar around standard public events. These may include spring beginnings, summer holidays or indeed any holiday that's in the public awareness. It's much easier to link your offers to existing events and thereby exploit your prospect's natural understanding of event or time-based scarcity.

Of course running your own events with a fixed date also naturally creates scarcity. I even use this strategy when I run webinars. Even if the webinars are recorded or replays, we've found that attendance and action rates on replays are higher because of the scarcity compared to a normal video. The video contains the same content – but is available anytime, so there is no urgency to consume it.

Limited Quantity

Another way of creating scarcity is to limit the quantity of the items available to purchase. If you were to offer a product or service, but only make it available for ten people rather than anyone and everyone who has the willingness and ability to pay, the perceived value of that service has immediately risen considerably.

This is because people understand that if only a few people can have something, then it must be more valuable. People generally want more of what they can not have or what is rare. So limiting the quantity of your products and service is a good way to raise its perceived value.

To really make the most of this form of scarcity, there are two different tactics you can use in conjunction for maximum effectiveness:

1. You can limit the availability of a product

2. You can increase the perceived demand for the product

There's not much point in saying 'only ten copies available' if nobody wants the product – this is still ten copies too many. Instead, it's helpful if you can demonstrate there is genuinely a high demand. A classic way of doing this is to say there are ten places available, and telling your list that you have sent this email to 20,000 prospects. You can immediately see the contrast between the ratio of prospects who might be interested in the offer and the limited amount of places available. You are creating true scarcity by leveraging the law of supply and demand.

One word of advice here - make sure that whatever you offer is true scarcity. Don't play games with your customers by telling them only one is available and then selling ten. This will destroy the trust and the reputation that you have built.

Open Door – Closed Door Scarcity

Another classic scarcity strategy is called 'open door – closed door'. Many products are available for a short time only. If you miss the 'open door' you have to join a waiting list for the next opportunity to get in. This works very well with membership sites that only open at specific times of the year or to a specific number of members. It also works very well with software products that are limited to a certain amount of users.

Using Deadlines

Here's a quick tip on using deadlines. I've found that deadlines between 24 and 72 hours work very well. Anything shorter doesn't allow people enough time to consider and anything longer means their desire will have waned. So if you use deadlines, use 24 to 72 hours for optimum results. These numbers come from many tests in different markets with multiple products, but please feel free to verify and test this in your own market with your own products and your list and let me know if your numbers differ.

Here is a real world example of a joint venture product I sold via a webinar. The webinar was on Wednesday evening, and the final deadline for ordering that product was midnight on Friday – two days later. On the Wednesday evening the webinar was broadcast we sold 59 copies. We sold another 74 copies Friday, mostly in the final hours just before the deadline. We sold hardly any on Thursday. Without that deadline these sales simply wouldn't have happened.

Contrast Frame

One final element that is particularly compelling in the creation of your offer is the use of a 'contrast frame'. A contrast frame is effectively where you're offering a product or service but you're providing a clear contrast for the price and value of the product or service by comparing it to another product, way of achieving similar results or normal price. So you end up selling the saving, not the price.

Selling Money at a Discount

Let's say you're selling a product that is based on an opportunity or an ability to make money in some form. One way that you can create a contrast frame is by what's called 'selling money at a discount'.

So if you're selling an opportunity where people can make £1,000s of pounds and you're selling it for £100, the people buying and investing in your product stand to gain way more than they could potentially lose by investing in your product. If I could offer you a way to get £1,000 and it only cost you £100, would you be interested to invest in that?

'Selling money at a discount' is one of the main ways that you can create a contrast frame for an opportunity-based product. Make the value clear to the purchaser of the product and make sure you give a reason why you're selling it below that price.

Selling the Intangible

Another means of creating a contrast frame is to sell intangible values. If I'm selling a product that will allow you to spend more time at home with your family, that is intangible. What indeed is the value to you of being able to spend more time at home with your family and children, compared to being away from home?

It's impossible (therefore it's an intangible value) to put a value on the time that you spend with your family but clearly it's of extreme value to many people. So, if my product can help you experience some of these intangible benefits, I'll make sure I create a clear contrast frame to this meager investment I'm asking from you in return.

Research has shown that lifestyle benefits by far outweigh any financial gain that a product or service can ever promise. If you can promise intangible lifestyle advantages e.g. by obtaining freedom or more quality time with your loved ones, you can create an impression of a very small investment compared to the huge gain your customers can expect from your product or service.

Make it a bargain (But never cheap)

Another strategy you really want to employ when you're creating a contrast frame is to make it clear that your offer is never 'cheap' but always a 'bargain'. Those words may seem like mere semantics, but actually there is a chasm of difference in meaning between the two.

Create a Plausible Reason for a Discount

You always have to give a plausible reason for why your product is available at a special price and is such a bargain. There are a number of reasons that you can use.

The Marketing Test

A plausible reason for discounting your products is that you're running a marketing test. Simply explain that this is a one-time initial offer just to 'see how it goes'. The reason doesn't have to be particularly exceptional or special; it just has to be plausible. People will understand that you're testing something new.

Display Stock

Some time ago a good friend of mine was having a stand at an exhibition. He had display copies from his home study course to sell at the show. After the show had finished he sold off the remaining display copies at a plausible discount. When the orders flooded in, he ran out of display copies. What did he do? He sent 'brand new' copies at the same discounted price with an apologetic letter asking people if they didn't mind receiving a new rather than a display copy. As far as I know, nobody sent the new version back!

'Beta' Testing

There is also a strategy to offer people the opportunity to 'beta test' your product. The word 'beta' is used from the software world and means before the product is ready for official release. Beta software versions typically might have some small 'bugs' or problems that need to be resolved.

So when you offer 'beta access' to people on your membership site, it implies that it won't be 100% ready and that is why you're happy to discount it. I also call it the 'Rough Round The Edges' offer. It serves two purposes, you can relieve yourself from having to produce the perfect product and your customers can enjoy a discount.

3. Cultivate a Buying Audience

The third part to lasting Expert Success is your ability to cultivate a buying audience. I call it 'audience' because I as an Expert and leader you have to communicate a message, which requires a willing, attentive audience. And it's not enough to just have an audience, you must focus on cultivating a buying audience.

When looking for a verb to go with 'Buying Audience' I settled on 'Cultivate', as it expresses care and nurture and also suggests that it will take some time to achieve. That is the reality of any relationship, but there are simple steps you can take and ideas you can adept to cultivate your own 'buying audience'.

3.1 Develop a Loyal Following

There are many reasons why developing a loyal following makes business sense. One main reason is that a loyal following will help you increase lifetime customer value, because loyal followers become repeat purchasers.

And it is common knowledge that looking for new customers and acquiring them is an expensive undertaking compared to selling to your existing loyal customers.

Every business has a small percentage of customers that can be classified as hyper-responsive. This means they buy your products at every opportunity, which produces a sky-high lifetime customer value. This is a key reason why it's important to create new products, have recurring products and ascending coaching levels.

These are the customers that will give you the greatest profits from your entire customer base. So it's obviously important to find out who they are, how they found you and talk to them regularly. Ask them what they're looking for and give them what they want (and need).

Brand Loyalty Avoids You Being 'Price-Shopped'

Another great reason to develop a loyal following is that you can avoid customers shopping you on price alone. Once you have built some trust and have started to develop loyalty with your brand and values, price will not be the most important criteria for making a purchasing decision. Your followers will prefer to buy from you over any competitor even if the price is not as competitive.

If you're currently running a business where price is the main factor that decides a customer's purchase, then you have a problem. Because there will always be some business owner dropping their prices for one or the other reason. In the long term, price is not a lasting competitive advantage.

That is why you have to focus on creating loyalty through consistent brand building.

The Evolution of 'Brand'

Every consumer has a relationship with the products and brands they buy. It's important to know where you rank with your customers and then to aim to move into level 3, 4 or 5 to maximize the effective of brand loyalty.

1. Brand Absence

Customers don't care what they buy. Price and convenience drive the purchasing decision.

2. Brand Awareness

Customers notice that there is a brand connected to the product or service. It is not the primary driver of the purchasing decision, but might influence it. Price is still the primary driver.

3. Brand Preference

The buyer will buy brand A over brand B. At this stage price moves into a secondary consideration. The consumer associates with the brand and has a conscious feeling of belonging.

4. Brand Insistence

At this stage people will buy the brand they are looking for or buy nothing. Common in fashion and food. Price plays a lesser role in the purchasing decision. As long as what they are looking for is in the range of products, they will not leave the safety of their brand. This normally comes with identifying yourself with the values of the brand and a strong sense of belonging to the tribe.

5. Brand Advocacy

People have such a strong sense of belonging. They will spend their time, attention and money to influence others to buy the brand and become part of the movement or tribe. Of course they own all the products in the product line and can't stop sharing how these products and the tribe have changed their lives for the better.

We all Need To Belong...

One of our basic human needs is to belong. We are tribal by nature. It has guaranteed the survival of the human race and is hard wired into our DNA. You can use this human need to belong and start to think about how you can create your own tribe or community.

When I ask my audiences what compelled them to join me and my company over other companies, I always get very similar responses. In reality they could have chosen to learn marketing and expert positioning and business skills from other companies as well. But they have chosen me based on my goals, values and history. Just to be clear – there are many folks who will not want to work with me for the same reason that others absolutely only want to work with me!

We already covered unique positioning and creating polarity (the marmite effect) earlier, but it's evident that your followers, clients and members will associate with the values and stories you create.

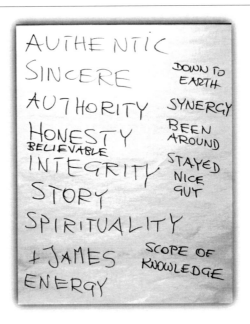

Here is a photo of a flip chart page from a recent Mastermind retreat. I asked them why they chose me and my program over other coaches and programs available to them. It is a good sign that what you stand for (your company values) is reflected in what your students/market/customers believe you stand for.

Let's look at an example from the world of corporate branding. Harley Davidson. They've carefully cultivated a loyal, passionate following where price doesn't feature in any of the main reasons why people want to own one of their coveted motorbikes. More important is the sense of belonging to an elite group of individuals that self-identify via their purchases and through their brand association.

This is not about going from A to B on two wheels! Belonging to an elite group gives purpose and confidence. Price is not in the top reasons why people choose a 'Harley'. Can you emulate this in your business?

Why do people follow?

In my own life I have joined a religious meditation group at age 21 and followed that particular Guru for almost twenty years. It was a very important part of my life and I was totally immersed in the group. There was a strong sense of belonging and identification with the mission and the movement.

So when I look back at my experience with this group I asked myself some pertinent questions: Why did I pay attention in the first place? Why did I follow? Why did I continue to follow? Why did I leave after twenty years? What I have found to be the reasons for this particular group are true for all groups and tribes.

So let's have a brief look at the three key reasons people follow and see how you can use this knowledge to build your own tribe or following.

Authority

The first is 'Authority'. People are constantly looking for leadership or advice. It stems from the need to look for guidance and help to survive and thrive in our complex society. Authority can come from knowledge, position, birth, status, skills or gifts. (And of course a combination of any of these).

The whole idea of Expert Success is that anyone with average skills and knowledge can become the authority in their niche or market.

Affinity

Another reason why people follow others is 'affinity'. In simple terms people like people who are like themselves. Perhaps they have a similar background, similar values or similar goals. People of similar backgrounds will naturally and unavoidably identify themselves with their peers.

This is why it's so important that you share your story about the struggles and breakthroughs and your personal journey. That provides information about your values and background that people can associate and connect with.

We all look for inspiration in our leaders, but we also look for people we can identify with and learn from. This is why it's so crucial you create a unique voice and a high-quality personal online brand. This is what communicates what you stand for and what you stand against so that people can quickly feel an 'affinity' with the image that you have created.

Celebrity

The third main reason why people follow others is 'celebrity'. We live in an age that's obsessed with celebrity culture. The assumption is that the attention, audience and money associated with the celebrity lifestyle will bring the meaning and purpose people are looking for.

I have had many entertaining incidents where people want to have their photo taken with me at various events. Just recently I was talking to a lady from a local paper and she recognised me from one of my speaking gigs. When a friend of hers asked who I was, she was almost embarrassed and said: 'Don't you know who he is?' - this is what I mean by 'minor celebrity' status (I also call it bubble celebrity, as it is only true in a small isolated group or audience).

There is no reason to get an ego about this sort of 'celebrity status'. It's just a tactic to help you become more successful faster and help more people.

Creating Loyalty

In my vocabulary loyalty is closely linked to trust, and it ties in with the creation of a long-term following. Therefore, you can do a lot to encourage and reward the loyalty of your followers and your audience. Loyalty is an emotional and illogical concept. If you can build a connection with people, with their desires, their fears and their deep emotions, then you will create loyalty for your own personal brand and create repeat buyers.

As an example, I offer special discounts for existing customers (and actually different levels of discounts depending on their loyalty and spend with me!) for our products and services. I also offer renewal discounts to reward loyalty (which just makes plain sense as you don't have the cost of acquiring a new customer).

Much of a person's loyalty will come from commitment over a period of time and the repetition of rituals and messages. Just take a US citizen's loyalty to their flag compared to other countries. It is part of every kids daily ritual to pledge allegiance to the flag – so by the time they are grown up they have 'practiced' loyalty.

Get Attention

Attention - the most valuable currency of all...

Attention is the most valuable currency and marks the beginning of every possible transaction or relationship. Science has shown that attention is of huge significance to human beings. In fact, it's a major contributing factor to survival - so it's pretty important.

There have been medical studies conducted in the twentieth century whereby new born babies have received no attention (or affection) but only the necessary food and water to survive. Shockingly - they all died within their first year. This seems to suggest that attention is an actual necessity for humans to survive. That explains why it's such an important thing for us to receive. That is why a big part of running a successful tribe or following is awarding attention and recognition.

Living in an 'ADD World'

When I was a kid ADD (Attention Deficit Disorder) didn't exist. At least it wasn't diagnosed or medicated! Today it seems everyone's got ADD!

We live in a world and in an age where we're overwhelmed with options and complexity. We now have hundreds of television channels where previously we only had three or four. The same is true in almost every area of life! The internet and the 'always on' generation has only exacerbated our condition!

The result of this overwhelm is that we increasingly don't know where to turn for guidance and advice. Everywhere we go there are new opportunities to distract us.

Astonishingly, one study reports that the average person in the USA views more than 3,000 ads per day thanks to TV, the Internet, advertising billboards and magazines. If it is true that our human mind can only pay attention to seven to nine signals or information sources at any one time, and thousands of them are competing for our attention every day, you can imagine what sort of 'filtering' is taking place!

Having a loyal following means having a 'direct line' to people's attention, so you don't have to compete against all the other channels over and over again. And having that trust and brand means that you don't have to re-establish it every time you want to communicate. It gets even better, as your followers will search for your message amongst the noise because they know it will provide comfort and familiarity!

With people's short attention spans and increased filtering mechanisms, you have to be clear what you'll actually do once you've got their attention.

Remember AIDA?

Attention is the first step of the classic four-step approach to sales and influence. It stands for Attention, Interest, Desire, and Action – the four stages of any sales process. It's no accident that attention is the first of the four steps. Indeed, it's a pre-requisite before moving on to the others.

How To move from attention to interest

Throughout every moment in time human beings are looking out for themselves and asking 'what's my benefit, what is my gain and why should I do this?'

So once you've reached out and got people's attention you have to quickly make sure that you can create interest in the person and tell them what it is you can do for them.

How To move from Interest to Desire

Thirdly, it is now time to evoke desire by showing people what life will be after they have received your answer, solution or consumed your product.

How To move from Desire to Action

Now that you have evoked a desire, the last step is to tell people exactly what to do next i.e. a clear and simple call to action.

Attracting attention – the conflict

Here's where an inner conflict for most human being starts. From early childhood on we've been told to avoid getting attention, whether in the classroom, or later on in the workplace. We are always told it's best not to attract attention and not to stand out. Our society conditions us to just blend in. This is reflected in the way we dress, the way we behave and our social conduct.

We're afraid of attention because it's scary, because it means possibly being a non-conformist, being shunned or being excluded from groups, tribes or society.

At the same time we worship people who have managed to get attention – leaders, experts, authorities and celebrities. This is where our deep fascination comes from, because we know that those people have overcome an intrinsic and built-in fear to stand out. So now that we know where the conflict starts – let's see what we can do to resolve it.

Resolving the conflict

Here are a few things you can do right now. Stop thinking that 'big is bad' and stop thinking that 'being wealthy is linked with being bad'.

We are conditioned to associate financial success with illegal or immoral behaviour (otherwise how come that the majority of good, hard working people are broke!). This mentality underpins our conditioning in society. The United Kingdom is especially well known for shunning success and has a strong culture of supporting the underdog. Compare this to the US, where it is part of their belief that anyone can become a millionaire in the 'land of opportunity'.

'The tall poppy syndrome' is just one of the ways to describe such behaviour. You must overcome your fear to rise above the rest and be that tall poppy and stand out from the crowd.

The secret of consistency

Consistency attracts attention. The reason is that it takes time for a message to be received in the market place. So be wary of the 'shiny object syndrome' e.g. looking for the missing piece, that 'secret sauce' or the missing ingredient that will make you successful. You've got to keep sharing the 'message' and the 'promise' - even if you think everybody knows it by now! There is comfort in consistency and people value certainty.

And because the majority of people don't have a clear plan of action about what they would like to achieve, your clarity and plan will attract their attention.

You are different and you have a plan - let them know! If you do what everyone else does, you'll be getting what everyone else gets! And you and I already know that this is not what you want!

Many people have made this point throughout history. Earl Nightingale, considered the father of the modern personal development industry, said 'in the absence of all other criteria, do the opposite of what the majority does because the majority are always wrong'.

John Francis Tighe's famous quote 'In the land of the blind, the one eyed man is King', similarly speaks to a concept of standing out from the crowd and also illustrates that even one eye is more than sufficient to be the leader in a land where the rest has no vision!

Mark Twain's quote: 'Observe the masses and do the opposite' simply states that the masses are always wrong. Think about it for a moment. You don't want what the masses have so you shouldn't do what the masses do. Most people don't have the lifestyle that you desire, they don't run the businesses you'd like and they don't have the income you desire.

How to get started

Communicating your message consistently and offering a clear plan to follow will attract people's attention. Here are a few ideas of what kind of message or plan I am thinking of.

Do Something that Solves a Problem

This is one of the key reasons why you are in business anyway. One definition of a business is that it 'solves problems at a premium'. Whether you run a restaurant, a local housing association or you're a coach or trainer, you always solve specific problems in return for money.

Most people in life are afraid, stressed, bored and lonely. If you can help them escape from where they are now, help them get away from the stress of financial worries or other insecurity, help them get excited at least momentarily, then you have a key ingredient of a valuable business proposition.

The 4 Core Markets

There are four key areas the people want help with. Literally all information marketing and coaching businesses operate in one (or multiples) of these markets.

1. Money - moving from Poverty to Wealth. This includes making money, getting out of debt, accumulating more of it, investing it...

2. Health - moving from Sickness to Health. Includes the diet industry, weight loss, getting more energy, curing of diseases, maintaining health, fitness...

3. Relationships - moving from Loneliness to Togetherness. Finding a partner, improving existing relationships, sexuality, coping with separation, self development...

4. Salvation - moving from Damnation to Salvation. All the self development world, spiritual and religious teachings, alternative therapies, the whole industry of finding purpose...

Making a bold promise n any of these four markets and it'll be easy for you to attract attention.

Study How Others Get Attention

If you want to get inspiration and guidance then look at how others are getting attention. It's healthy to look outside your market, so look outside your comfort zone and see how they do it.

One of my key observations is that you're a customer yourself so what are you paying attention to currently? And why? Just spend a few hours over the next few days. Observe and write down what you're paying attention to - in the newspaper, in the news, online, in your RSS reader - what is it that you're paying attention to and ask yourself - why am I paying attention to it?

Is it because of the curiosity that it creates? Is it because of the desires it promises to fulfill? Is it the controversy it sparks?

Then ask yourself - 'how did they do it, how did they get my attention?' Because you're like every other human being, with desires to be fulfilled. Here's the lesson - if they can get your attention then you too can get the attention of others!

Look who's 12 months ahead

If you're paying attention to people and asking yourself why and how they've done something, here is the next step. Model them. Break down how they do what they do and see how you can do something similar or better.

Look at people who are not too far ahead of you and who have similar circumstances to you.

'Forget Branson and Trump'

Here's some advice you'll not hear very much: 'Forget Branson and Trump'. I am actually tired of hearing people permanently quoting what Branson's thinking and what Trump's doing because they are simply so many years down the line that a lot of their habits, a lot of their ways of doing business will not apply to where you are today at all.

Don't get me wrong: I've read their books and there's some cool stuff in there. They have definitely managed to get attention and they are prime examples of Expert positioning and the power of personal branding, but I don't want you to get frustrated and despondent by comparing yourself and failing to live up to people like Branson and Trump. It's taken an exceptional combination of human qualities, market conditions and timing to create those empires.

A Case Study on Getting Attention for free (First Steps)

Here is how I got started: In 2004 I started speaking in other peoples events for free, 15 minutes at a time, offering some good advice, something slightly controversial and interesting solving a problem most people in the room had. I did that for free and I didn't sell any product or service. But I started to build a loyal following by simply giving consistently good information.

Soon after that I was able to sell information, to a list of just 500 people that I'd built up over six months. It cost me nothing apart from some time investment. This is a strategy you can easily copy and follow. Find people who run events in your industry, offer to speak for free, share some good information without asking for anything in return and start from there. Within two short years I ran my own events and the rest, as they say is history.

Just in case you were wondering exactly what I was sharing back in 2004 to a group of property investors? My talk was 'How to get a part time PA for £1 a call in 15 minutes or less!' I could spend a whole chapter on 'copy writing' - but I hope you'll agree that it evokes curiosity and a desire to find out more.

Patience Required

Often people are not patient enough. As long as you keep using your voice and style and keep sharing good information you'll get noticed – eventually. It's actually better to grow your following organically.

Keeping Attention

I've shared a few examples and strategies on how to get some initial attention from your market place. Let's focus on how to keep attention from your followers how can you move that attention into transactional value for you.

Continuous communication

To keep people's attention it's important that you have continuous communication with your prospects or your customers. Attention is just like advertising: once is not enough.

Google's 'Zero Moment Of Truth' shares a new model of marketing that talks about the increased number of touch points needed to drive prospects to action.

It appears that there are more and more follow-up steps needed to lead to a transaction. You may have heard about the seven points of contact required, but a recent study by Google suggests that this number has gone up to 10 or even 13.

Whatever the number it means that you'll have to follow-up a whole lot more than you do right now to get people to know you're even there!

Be in the forefront of people's minds

Here is a key concept - you want to stay in the forefront of your customer or prospect's mind. For example, if you were a plumber you want to be in the forefront of the customers mind so that when there is an emergency happening your customer immediately thinks of you rather than someone else.

'People buy when they are ready to buy...'

A critical point to remember is that people don't buy when you're ready to sell, they buy when they're ready to buy. Bill Glazer says that the GKIC (Glazer Kennedy Inner Circle) coaching model he used to run had 263 touches with their customers per year. If you take off weekends, that's literally every day of the year!

Using Automation

Now before you freak out, this is not all done manually – you don't have to spend every day of the year following up with your customers.

Here are a couple of simple automation tools and tips that will help you stay in touch with your prospects and keep their attention automatically.

Using Autoresponders

We use http://infusionsoft.com as our customer database, manage follow up sequences for prospect customers with multiple media, e.g. newsletters, CDs or products, as well as for our shopping cart to process orders online and by phone.

But if you are just looking for specialist autoresponder software you can use http://1dollartrial.aweber.com. This will help you to create those email sequences too. Set it up once, forget it and let it run.

You will need a good mix of strategic sequences and ad-hoc, one-off promotions.

Quality and consistency

It's not only important to communicate continuously, it's also important to produce quality products and content. Here are some examples of the types of content you could be creating.

Become a contributor

Become a regular contributor to other people's businesses. This simple strategy is especially valuable to attract potential prospects and future customers.

In the online world you can do that by guest blogging or by becoming a guest columnist in an online newsletter. Pick the leaders and just ask.

When you produce content or products they can be one of three types:

1. One-off products, content for specific promotions.

2. Seasonal products, content for specific promotions. Your marketing calendar should be based around events

3. Evergreen products, content for specific promotions, which means that you can promote those products or services or content all year round.

The Printed Newsletter

A simple way to keep in continuous communication with your prospects and customers is to publish your own newsletter. My 'Expert Success' newsletter is a good example. Published monthly, it allows me to communicate with my coaching clients.

It allows my team to get and keep my students' attention (undivided!), especially as it's printed and sent in the post. It ensures we get more one-to-one time with our customers, build better rapport, share value and success stories and communicate what's going on in our world.

I believe a newsletter can add to pretty much any business no matter what products or service they provide. Now you may be thinking that it's easier to do an online rather than offline newsletter, and you're probably right and from the few people who get round to actually doing a newsletter, most just do an online version!

Here is another reason why I love the printed newsletter concept: People love to collect and store things. We even provide a newsletter folder for all new coaching clients and they collect our 'Expert Success' newsletter and archive them. This means we have a much longer time connection with our customers.

The newsletter also allows you to showcase testimonials, results, case studies, new products and even produce inserts for promotions.

This turns the newsletter into a marketing and sales tool as well, and your clients will even pay for it!

Here at 'Expert Success' we combine it with a monthly audio CD that caters for multiple learning styles. From our analytics we know that the CD is a big part of the appeal of the monthly newsletter.

If you're not sure how to produce a newsletter or where to get it done, there are hundreds of fulfillment house that can take the job of printing, packaging and sending these newsletters to your database. When you first get started you can handle the small numbers you'll need yourself with your normal inkjet or laser printer. That's how I got started.

A couple more tips on newsletters

The first one is that you can always include a marketing message in your newsletter. If it's printed you can include that without any additional cost or postage, which, in effect is free promotion for you.

The second tip is to make sure that the content in your newsletter is not only 'how to do' information. It's important that at least 40% of the content is personal and related to your life. This connects with your customers in the ways that we've already talked about. This is one of the very best opportunities to build the connection that fosters long-term customer loyalty.

Thirdly, put a price on it. That equates to the value your customers will perceive the newsletter to have. This is not a £1 paper or a £2 magazine. My 'Expert Success' newsletter and the 'Expert Success CD of the Month' are £27 each a month and are part of the value of the 'Expert Success Coaching' packages.

Increasing Attention

Let's explore to to get more! To grow your status and expert positioning, you'll need to learn how to increase the attention you're getting.

Wait for it ... Anticipation!

An important and underused strategy for increasing attention is to build anticipation. You can use this strategy for your prospects and customers alike ahead of the release of important information or future products.

This model is used in elaborate product launches but can also be used for pretty much anything message or announcement you have to make. Just build some excitement and curiosity and focus your tribes mind on a specific action and time frame.

Using open loops

When you create anticipation or you 'open a loop' in NLP terms, people are anxious to close that loop and will pay attention to what you say until the loop is closed. You can e.g. link every message to a future messages, which will keep your readers engaged and interested.

It's the same trick soap operas use to keep people watching! Multiple overlapping stories that open new loops and create cliffhangers. That's how they get their audiences hooked!

They 'miss' messages

I hate to break it to you, but not every one of your customers and prospects will open every email and receive each and every one of your messages. So the opportunity to send four or five messages about one event and build the anticipation will really just make sure that you capture a much larger part of your prospects or customers.

Leveraged contacts and finding a cause

Another great way to increase attention is to seek out what I call leveraged contacts. I've spent the last couple of years seeking out authorities in related or similar markets. Once I find them, I try to get their attention, align myself with them in one way or the other and start to work with them in strategic partnerships.

Within weeks of joining the Peace One Day patrons I was invited on stage at one of their Events.

Let me share a recent example of that strategy: I was looking for a cause I can support as a company, and I shortlisted some charities. One that stood out for me was 'Peace One Day' (http://peaceoneday.org). It's not the cause though that stood out for me, it was the existing supporters and their patrons program that got my attention. I wanted to tap into Jeremy Gilley's amazing network of celebrities, authorities and successful entrepreneurs in my market.

I would urge you to seek out similar alignments and relationships to help you build your positioning and to increase attention. Of course my alignment with those celebrities and groups will build more attention for me in the industry as I position myself as an even greater authority and expert.

3.2 Maximise Customer Revenue

A Simple Formula

Once you've developed a loyal following, the next stage is to capitalise on that loyalty by maximising your customer revenue.

In essence there are just three ways to increase your customer revenue in any businesses: increase order volume, increase order frequency and increase transaction value. In other words, your aim is to do at least one, ideally all three of the following things:

1. Sell to more people

2. Sell more frequently to those people

3. Sell a higher transaction amount to those people

Many businesses focus on just the first of those three – finding more people to sell to. And they are struggling forever chasing and acquiring new customers.

If you asked a business owner what would fix his problems, most of them will answer that they 'need more leads'. They think that their problems will be solved by more and new customers.

As a consequence of that they neglect the other two areas, which is to increase the frequency of their customers' purchases and to increase the order value per transaction.

The latter two ways are an easier, quicker, cheaper and more predictable way to increase not only revenue, but also profits in your business.

I'll share a few proven and tested simple techniques you can use immediately that are guaranteed to bring you results. Don't be fooled by their simplicity though! Many of my students and clients have seen dramatic increases – I am talking about doubling and tripling their sales – just from using one of the strategies I am about to share. They are simple to do, yet most people and businesses fail to implement them.

List Segmentation

A good friend of mine was recently flown to the US and was paid a handsome six figure sum to consult with a multi million dollar company. Within just a few months their sales sky rocketed! I was curious to find out what 'secret ingredient' he recommended to his client that was able to increase their conversion by 900%! You guessed it - simple list segmentation. So now that you know just how powerful this can be!

As I just mentioned earlier, two ways to increase customer revenue is selling more frequently to your existing customers and to increase the value per transaction.

You can achieve both these when you segment your list. You should speak very differently to your prospects compared to your customers or indeed your hyper-responsive customers. The more you tailor your communication to various segments of your audience, the better your conversion and your results will be.

Imagine your list like your personal connections. You have family, close friends, acquaintances. There are also people you never personally met who know of you. And it goes without saying that you would talk differently and say different things to any of these groups. When you meet people for the first time, the stories you tell, the language you use, the information you share, will be very different to people you have a long standing relationship with, have built trust with and who know about your background.

Your business communication is just the same. You'll have to tailor the communication to people who are new to you and your business compared to people who are experienced in what you stand for and have experience and had results with your products and services.

For example, your prospects may not yet understand some of the concepts and terminology that you use with your customers. You have to make sure you take time to introduce new concepts they don't know so you don't alienate them. Also, before they make their first purchase, your prospects will need more convincing, might need more testimonials and social proof. Your existing customers just need to know where the 'Buy Now' button is. If you talk to all of your audience at the same time in the same voice – you'll leave tons of money on the table.

I have used Infusionsoft now for four years in all my businesses. It allows me to segment my database in multiple ways. We can find segments of our database by transactions, volume, interest, and so on. If you have low open rates of your emails and communication, one of the reasons will be that your communication is too generic and not specific enough.

Even a simple tool like AWeber allows you to create separate sublists based on actions like subscribes or optins.

The recent rise and explosive growth of Google+ is, in my opinion, partly based on Google's ability to quickly and easily share different information with different 'circles', making it the easiest social media platform to talk to segments of your whole audience.

Multi-Step Multimedia Campaigns

The second simple strategy is to use multi-step campaigns using multiple media or channels.

You'll have to create these campaigns for at least your prospect and customer segment of your list. I highly recommend using multi-step campaigns with both your prospects and customers segments.

Here are just a few other ideas for these sort of campaigns:

Product Stick Campaigns

Create 'stick campaigns' for every product or service you sell. This will ensure that people who bought the product are encouraged to consume, and learn how to get the most from your products.

Here are some simple content ideas for your stick campaigns:

1. Let them know about other people who've bought your product or services so they feel good about their purchase.

2. Tell them about a specific feature or benefit and tell them where to find it in the product.

3. Send them a FAQ message to answer questions they might possibly have.

4. Encourage them to contact you or your office with any questions about the product.

Many businesses do a great job up and until they sold you their stuff. Then suddenly it's as if they disappeared from the face of the earth. This will trigger buyers' remorse, increase refunds and other inconveniences for your business.

The biggest loss though is that if customers don't consume your product, they won't get the benefit or promised life change, making them much less likely to buy from you again or recommend your company or product.

Event Campaigns

If you're in a business that runs events or workshops make sure you allow enough time ahead of those events for these multi-step campaigns to do their job.

Apart from event marketing campaign I always create a 'reversed sequence' meaning a set of communication to have people show up. Even if they bought the ticket, they have to show up to benefit from the event (and be able to buy the next step in your staircase). So showing up is crucial!

Beyond email marketing

Most people use e-mail because it's easy and cheap. Some are perhaps now adding a bit of social media with their e-mail marketing, but to get and keep people's attention you need to work harder and smarter than the rest and do what a lot of people aren't prepared to do.

> *TopTip: Subscribe to your peers to keep an eye on what they are doing. (You won't be surprised to hear that most of them don't do very much at all).*

Why not use offline marketing as well as online marketing? Get on the phone, send out letters, send out postcards, use text message marketing - do whatever it takes to stand out and get people's attention. Don't worry about communicating too many times or too much.

A very successful colleague of mine has communicated more than twenty times with me about his £997 event. From automated and personal phone calls to emails, from webinars and multiple postcards, including some 'lumpy mail' items. And although I wasn't the least interested in the beginning, by the time I received the fifteenth piece of communication, I almost bought the darn thing!

Direct Mail

One heavily underused medium is direct mail. Today's technology makes it very easy, efficient and effective. Services like http://cfhdocmail.com or http://imail.co.uk are UK based and deliver millions pieces of mail every week. You simply upload your design, upload your database segment and press go. There is no minimum quantity and it'll cost you less than a second class stamp!

The power of multimedia is that you'll catch far more people by using a variety of other media rather than only one. People will buy when they are ready to buy, so being able to be in front of them in many ways, in different areas of their life, not just while they are in front of the computer, but also through their letterbox, or on the phone, means that you connect with them in different ways.

SMS Text Marketing

Another media worth mentioning is text marketing or SMS marketing. If you haven't tried it yet, have a play. It works really well for me. I have tested and used SMS marketing for the last four years now, but recent new software and players in the market have made it even easier to use this medium.

One of the best results for me is when I use SMS messaging to remind people of webinars, send them username and password confirmations or generally remind them of events. Advanced applications can integrate with your database so you can send messages directly as a result of certain actions and totally automate this.

I also do the marketing for a small local massage therapy business, and every time I send out a message I generate revenue. It takes less than 5 minutes to send a message which generates at least £100 in additional sales every time.

Product Sales Strategies

There are a couple of different ways of selling more stuff to the same people. These next few product sales strategies deal with order frequency and transaction value increases.

Up-Selling and Cross-Selling

The first concept is called up-selling. Up-selling is based on the idea that when people have made a decision to buy your product, they are more inclined to buy a related product at the same transaction.

You'll be familiar with the idea of if you ever ordered some food at a well known fast food chain. A friendly request from a well trained employee will ask you if 'You want fries with that!' or 'go large' – these are classic up-sell questions; you have made your decision to buy and then you're asked if you would like to upgrade or increase your order. These two questions are asked millions of times a day – do you think some people accept to offer?

From my own research I know that a third of all people are willing to make a further 30% purchase right at the point of purchase, which means that your overall purchase volume will increase by about 10% simply by asking the question.

What is also noteworthy is that although the upsell might amount for just 10% of the sales volume, but it is almost 100% profit! This is because you've already acquired the customer on the initial transaction and many times the upsell has little or no additional fulfillment cost.

Another way of increasing product sales is to cross-sell. Amazon are masters of cross-selling and next time you're ordering, I'd urge you to have a look and watch Amazon's list of 'people who bought the same as you also bought other items'.

I can't even recall the amount of times I've added more items to my basket from that suggested list which is highly targeted, highly relevant, and allows me to get even more value. I have absolutely no resentment towards Amazon for suggesting related products, so you shouldn't feel bad about offering related products or services that can help your customer get even more value and learn more about their chosen subject.

The key concept here is that products are 'related'. Amazon is able to do this thanks to its enormous database of customer transactions – it intelligently understands what products are naturally the most related to others. But even without being Amazon, you can surely work out related products or services that you can offer as an up-sell or cross-sell or recommend what other customers have bought together.

Down-Selling

A similarly powerful concept is the down-sell. If you offer a product or service to your prospects or existing customers and they decline your offer, why not offer them a smaller purchase or a similar product at a lower price?

Price could have been the one reason why they did not buy. Your prospects might have seen the benefits and the merit of your product or service and they might have liked everything about it except the price.

Therefore by offering them a down-sell, which is a similar opportunity at a lower cost, you can increase your revenue dramatically.

For example, if you were selling physical CDs for a product you could offer to sell the digital MP3 version instead for a lower price. Interestingly enough, I've found that once people have said yes to the down-sell you can again up-sell them, as they are now in 'buying mode'.

A top tip is to offer the same price, but possible as a payment plan, making the transaction more viable for more prospects.

Bundling

Another great way of increasing customer revenue is by bundling products together. Having three, four or five products in a certain market that all sell at a specific value, you can, at any time offer a person who is about to order one of your products the other three or four and bundle them at a massive discount.

This will help you to increase your order value and get your customer to consume more of your products. If you combine this with the earlier mentioned product stick campaign you'll have a lot more and happier clients and more revenue in the bank.

A Key Mindset Shift

'Most people try to find customers to sell products to. What you want to do instead is to sell products in order to find customers.'

The key is to find the right customers that you can generate a long-term relationship with and that come back and buy from you again and again. What most people do is to try and sell one off items to as many as people as they can – without discrimination.

Now that you understand that key difference, implement some of the aforementioned in your business and watch the difference in your results!

Referral Strategies

Another underused strategy to help maximise customer revenue is to use referral strategies. Want a quick and easy tip? Just ask. Ask your customers to refer you to other prospects. Your happy customers will most likely know people similar to themselves. This means they have similar needs and will be great prospects for your product or service.

You can go further and incentivise your customer's to refer, e.g. with discounts or prizes. You'll see more advanced strategies later on when I talk about profitable partnerships. Affiliates, Joint Venture Partners and Strategic Partners are just elaborate forms of referral strategies. The internet and different software packages make accounting for these referral incentives is very easy! But before you spend time and money setting up affiliate programs and planning strategic partnerships, do ask your customers if they know someone who could benefit from your product or services.

I suggest you ask right at the point of making the sale. If you do it well, your customers will simply accept that this is a natural course of action they need to take. This means that at the point of ordering, you ask for the details of other like-minded people who would benefit from the product and services that you offer. Many businesses have been built by this 'one customer refers another customer' strategy. Once you have one customer you continually get at least one other referral. You then just keep going and going.

Track, Measure & Improve

One of the biggest sources of hidden revenue in your business s to track what is actually going on. Online marketing tools and analytics software makes it easy to track and measure what actually happens on the journey of your prospects all the way to your customer all the way to working out the life time value of a customer to your business.

One of the most important metrics that should define what you do in your marketing is the ROI - Return On Investment. Absolutely every marketing activity you do should be measurable as a direct return on the investment you have made. This is the underlying principle of direct response marketing.

Once you have a clear understanding of your numbers, including cost per sale, lifetime customer value and transaction averages, you can employ more advanced strategies like 'self-liquidating offers' or SLOs. This is where you're happy to forgo profit on the first item people buy, because you know the ratio and value of the next transactions that your customers will commit to.

Only do this if you know your conversion numbers and have run a stable business for a while. If you are starting out, make sure every part of your product staircase is profitable in its own right.

Key Metrics to track

Email Tracking

With email tracking, the two key metrics you need to know are the open rates of your emails and the click through rates on the call to action links inside your emails. Most email packages provide you with an open rate estimate. Look at how to use trackable links inside your emails along with software that measures how many people click on that link.

Once people have clicked on that link inside the email there are a few metrics around lead generation you need to understand.

Opt-Ins and Conversion Tracking

If you drive people to an opt-in page, you need to know how many of the people who land on the page actually part with their name and email address – this constitutes the opt-in rate of that page.

The next important metric of your leads is how many of those leads are converted into a sale. Those numbers are highly important and need to be measured so that you can optimize and improve them.

This is referred to as the conversion rate of your sales pages. You need to know what the conversion rate is per 100 visitors to your sales page. So, if three people were to buy the product per 100 visitors that would be a 3% conversion rate.

Lifetime Customer Value

Another key metric to track in your business and in our clients businesses is lifetime customer value. Now this may be not easy to determine for you when you're a new business, and that lifetime customer value might increase over time, but track and measure what you can.

Make sure the life time value goes up over time. The average customer value can be a great metric to measure how good you're doing overall as a business.

Cost of Customer Acquisition

Once you know your lifetime customer value you can work out how much you are able to pay to acquire a new customer.

The higher the lifetime customer value, the more you can spend on acquiring a new customer. The more you make per customer, the more money you can spend on acquiring that customer. Which means that you can use marketing methods and channels that many of your competitors won't be able to touch.

You can see that tracking and measuring just a handful of key metrics will give you a massive advantage in your industry and put you well ahead of your competition.

TopTip: 'What you measure will improve.'

3.3 Attract Profitable Partnerships

The information in this chapter alone has generated more revenue for me and many of my peers than anything else. These strategies can literally 'sky-rocket' your business growth. Although you can use much of this information at any point of your business, the best leverage and results will come to you when you have created a good level of personal branding and have a strategic product staircase.

Leverage trust of others...

The key principle of working with partners is that you can leverage the trust that they have built with their audiences. Prospects that join your list from any partner promotion are highly qualified and are naturally more trusting. Using Product Launches and Joint Venture promotions can be a very quick way to grow your database. It's also scalable as there are many possible partners for you out there – in almost any market or niche.

If you are a startup or newer business, then this strategy is brilliant because it poses a very low risk and requires literally no upfront investment. The cost of acquiring customers is payable post sale and only per sale, not prospect.

I have made a deliberate distinction between three types of partners. The main difference between the three types is the complexity of creating and maintaining them, and the number of them in your business, but in essence they are all variations on the same idea - leveraging existing trust.

Affiliates

If you're not familiar with the term, affiliates are 'commission-only sales people'. They are people who generate leads and sales for your products yet they're only paid a percentage or commission once the sale has actually taken place. You have very limited risk in allowing affiliates to promote your products because you only pay them once you have been paid.

The only question is which platform you'll chose to make sure all the technicalities like creating unique links and affiliate resources like banners, emails, and so on are personalised and tracked. Any good affiliate software will provide the affiliate with detailed statistics of clicks, leads and sales and will give them a ledger of commission due.

http://Clickbank.com is possible the most widely known affiliate marketplace. It allows anyone to become an affiliate for free and start promoting literally tens of thousands of information products. You could even choose Clickbank to publish and host your products, and they take care of collecting your money, work out and pay your affiliates and pay you for a small commission.

I have used ClickBank to sell products and to promote them. Today I have a multi-tier affiliate program built in with our Infusionsoft application. It doesn't matter too much which platform you are using, as long as you start exploiting these hidden profits in your business.

One example from my own business is an affiliate promotion I ran with my good friend Steven Essa - 'The Webinar King'. I met Steven at an event in London where we both shared a stage. I liked what he had to offer, it was very complementary to the product and services I already had, and it was highly specialized. The affiliate promotion generated $54,000 in sales from a single webinar and I was paid a commission of $27,000 as a result.

Steven is happy because he has a whole range of new customers that he'll be working with for many years to come, I'm happy because of both the affiliate commission and because I was able to add more value to my list. Crucially, my customers are also happy because they've found more information that helps them build their businesses. It's an all around win-win-win situation.

When I launched the Blueprint Coaching Program, I had dozens of affiliates promoting the launch with me. As a result I added over ten thousand new prospects and almost one thousand customers to my database and I was able to generate over $250,000 in revenue. But even more important than the original revenue is that many of the people who invested in the Blueprint Coaching Program are still on my customer database today and still buy my products.

Joint Ventures

The second type of partnership is a Joint Venture. The Joint Venture partnership is different from the Affiliate Partnership because it is normally based on a reciprocal arrangement or agreement. Some of your Affiliates (mainly the more established businesses) will become Joint Venture Partners.

Here is how these deals normally work: 'I promote your product to my list and you pay me commission, then you promote my product to your list and I pay you commission'.

Because only a handful of people ever buy a product, there is also a positive side effect of JV (Joint Venture) promotions. Your list gets new, fresh names, who have not yet been exposed to your products and services. And with your newly acquired skills to build trust and nurture your prospects, many of them will become customers in due course.

Strategic Alliances

In some cases, Joint Venture Partners become Strategic Alliances. They are relationships that influence the direction of your business. That means that you adjust and consider joint goals and longer term plans to help each other grow your businesses.

You might be finding a Strategic Partner amongst your existing JV partners. One example in my business is Rob Moore and his companies Progressive Property and Unlimited Success. Rob and I met back in 2007 and we have been making money together ever since.

We have found a great synergy with my offering and his audience that we decided to plan a whole range of activities that helps both his and my businesses.

Setting up Affiliate Programs

Creating affiliate programs today is very easy as there are many software programs that offer you everything you need. This includes adding products, designing affiliate structures (how many levels) and creating custom affiliate links. iDevAffiliate and PostAffiliatePro are some of the most widely used stand alone packages, many of the database solutions like Infusionsoft and 1ShoppingCart have them built in or you can go to places like ClickBank.com.

Your affiliate program is a valuable product

Setting up the programs and choosing your software is outside the scope of this book, but once you've created your affiliate program you should treat it like one of your own valuable products.

As with your prospect and customer sequence we touched on earlier, your affiliates are effectively a database segment that needs unique and special communication. They are part of your team and you pay them money for making sales for you. So give them the attention they deserve and give them what they need!

You want to make sure you have follow-up sequences in place to help them, incentives to reward them and when you do product launches you look after them as you would look after your most valuable customers.

Be generous

In the online world, the average percentage commission for affiliates is around 50%. This might surprise you and might seem high, but digital products have a low cost of fulfillment, with high margins.

Things are very different if you affiliate to physical products. If you are an affiliate for someone like Amazon.com that sells mainly physical products you'd expect single digit percentage commissions if you refer sales.

So while it's great to be generous, make sure your business model can support the commissions you are offering. It's not a good idea to cut commissions in the future when you realize you can't afford them. Nobody likes a pay cut!

Leverage existing customers

You'll find 'hidden' affiliates in your existing customer base. You can make significant extra revenue for example from simple 'bring a friend' promotions. We run our 'Expert Success Partner' program for our products and services, which is free to join and which pays out generous commissions. The reason this strategy works so well is that an existing advocate of my brand or service brings a friend and I can leverage the trust of their relationship.

I have seen people feel bad to get paid commission on their friends purchases, and they end up giving the money back to their friends to - in effect - discount the purchase. I would encourage you to take the money! If you have benefitted from the program and your friend joins after evaluating it, you have every right to get a referral commission.

I would argue that I should get paid on every film, book or restaurant I recommend if there was a way to track it!

Setting up Joint Ventures

When I got started I had zero joint venture partners to call on. That is normal. I found that one of the easiest ways to find out who is a potential joint venture partner for you is to join joint venture competitions and launch competitions. Identify who the biggest players are in your market. Make a list and contact them. In the internet marketing world there is a site called http://JVnotifypro.com that keeps track of some of the biggest launches in the industry.

If you can make it into those 'JV Contests' league tables, then even better. You'll attract the attention of other players who will most likely contact you when they launch their next product.

It's NOT always about the money

Although it might come as a surprise, the money they could make from promoting you is not always the main criteria to make a decision on a JV; sometimes it will be the services you can offer to the joint venture partner, sometimes it'll be favors you can do for them or a person you can introduce them to.

Once you've built up some relationships, they last for years. Some of my JV relationships go back five or six years and have been worth hundreds of thousands of pounds to me. Like with other relationships, communications and arrangements get easier as you build trust over time.

One of the best ways to get noticed is to make sales for them first, then you can approach them for a possible joint venture. It also shows that you know about their products and are interested in what they do.

Often the best and easiest way to start a dialogue is to comment on their blogs and interact with them on Facebook or Twitter.

When people approach me I normally create little challenges or have some hoops I make them jump through. Nothing devious, just postponing a meeting twice or making them call back or write me a short proposal. You'll be amazed how many fall on the first hurdle! If they can't pass the first test, they'll never be a successful JV partner.

Think 'Co-Opetition'

When it comes to joint ventures you want to think 'co-opetition'. It means that you want to 'co-operate with your competition'. This concept is alien to traditional businesses where they're in fierce competition with each other, especially in local markets. But among the more enlightened service-based businesses, you want to have an abundant mindset and understand the very important concept that 'a buyer is a buyer is a buyer'.

Your buyers will almost certainly be consuming other material from other people in your industry and in fact, they'll almost certainly be consuming far more than you can produce on your own. So don't fight it, just run with it and make some more profit by joint venturing with the other players in your industry, even if their products are similar to your own.

Here's a great example from our industry, with two leading experts in the expert positioning industry, Eben Pagan and Brendan Burchard. Brendan did a promotion where he promoted Eben Pagan's Guru Blueprint.

Now this is a similar product to Brendan's own Expert Academy Blueprint Formula, but that doesn't matter. A buyer's a buyer and many people will gladly want to buy both products, so why shouldn't Brendan benefit by getting an affiliate commission from everyone who buy's Eben's product via his affiliate link?

Of course, in return, Eben will do the same thing. Both parties will make more sales and increase the size of their prospect databases via these reciprocal promotions. Fact is they have a different and unique positioning and attract a different client base.

Check what you're endorsing

Always, always check the product that you're promoting on behalf of a joint venture partner. Why am I so adamant about that? Because I made that very mistake a few years ago in a promotion that generated a lot of money for me, but that also cost me a lot in terms of grief. It was a lesson learned the hard way, but at least that's one mistake I'll never make again.

Choose well

This doesn't mean that you should joint venture with everybody in your industry. Do your due diligence as I mentioned before, but for the big players, the guys with big reputations and great products, why would you not have a go?

Some of these relationships take years to build and you can't expect immediate success with this strategy. But get started. One of the main reason why your first attempt might not be successful is that successful people have strategies and plans of their own in place. This means that knocking on their door requesting a promotion next week will not work because they most likely they have a marketing calendar (like I do now) and are already busy doing something else.

Identifying Strategic Alliances

Although they will develop naturally from joint ventures over time, you can be proactive and identify possible strategic partners in your marketplace that you might want to work within the next 12 -18 months. Start to get noticed, attend their events, buy their products, make some sales for them. Whatever it is to get closer to them, get the process started.

Buy yourself some new friends...

An amazing shortcut is to 'buy yourself' into mastermind groups or get into a mentoring relationship if the strategic partners you identified offer that. I used that very strategy in 2008 when I joined Dan Bradbury's Platinum Group. I wanted to work with him and he'd previously ignored my emails and any other attempt of contacting him.

Once I'd bought his highest priced product – his Platinum Group – I became his 'instant friend' and had access to him. It's years later now and we are still doing business together and have become friends.

When people join my Expert Success Inner Circle Mastermind you actually get a JV promotion to my list as part of the deal. Many Mastermind students have generated thousands of pounds of revenue from this opportunity.

Recently we changed our 'ideal customer profile' and moved more into the 'business world'. I found a group of business people that were already operating in that market, so my goal was simply to join that group.

Here's how I did it: a charity called 'Peace One Day' ran a one-day event promoting their £5,000 per year patrons program. I wanted to get noticed and decided to be a very prolific auction participant. As expected, by the end of the day I was everyone's new best friend in that 'inner circle' of well connected business owners.

Within just days I was consulting with a multi millionaire business owner who has founded the fastest growing franchise in the UK – pretty handy for my planned Expert Success License Program - and I was able to run some of my ideas by this experienced and successful guy.

By joining that group I am part of 30 to 40 business people all in the right peer group, all in the right markets to position me perfectly for my strategic goals for the next few years. I would urge you to do the same. For a small investment of £5,000, £10,000 or £20,000 you can buy relationships that you would otherwise have no access to.

Next Steps...

Congratulations if you have made it to here. You are already an exceptional individual – most people don't read books to the end!

I've done my best to explain the 3 step to Expert Success, the formula that's created many millions of pounds in revenue for many different businesses in many different industries.

Now it's down to you how to use this information and make it work for you.

How To Get In Touch...

Just email me personally at danielwagner@expertsuccess.com or email my office at office@expertsuccess.com

We have a range of products and services all designed to help you and your company do better! From workshops and coaching programmes to consultancies and keynotes. Get in touch and let us know how we can serve you best.

to YOUR Expert Success